# Shrub Roses, Climbers & Ramblers

# Shrub Roses, Climbers & Ramblers

Michael Gibson

*Illustrated with colour
photographs by the author*

COLLINS
St James's Place, London

William Collins Sons & Co Ltd
London · Glasgow · Sydney · Auckland
Toronto·· Johannesburg

First published 1981

© Michael Gibson 1981

ISBN 0 00 219013 3

Filmset by Jolly & Barber Ltd, Rugby

Colour reproduction by Adroit Photo-Litho Ltd, Birmingham

Made and printed in Great Britain by
William Collins Sons & Co Ltd, Glasgow

# Contents

# Acknowledgements

I would like to thank Jack Harkness for looking through the manuscript of this book for me and for making a number of very valuable comments and suggestions. At the same time, as we do not agree on everything – and which two writers on roses do? – responsibility for what appears in the finished book must be mine alone.

Although a large proportion of the colour pictures of roses were taken in my own garden, I would also like to make acknowledgement to other gardens where many of them were photographed. These include several belonging to the National Trust, including Sissinghurst Castle, Greys Court, Nymans, Hidcote Manor and Mottisfont Abbey, Wisley Gardens of the Royal Horticultural Society, Burford House, the garden of Mr and Mrs Jeremy Campbell-Grant in Worcestershire, and above all the gardens of the Royal National Rose Society near St Albans in Hertfordshire. I hope the pictures will be an encouragement to everyone to visit those among them that are open to the public, so that they can see shrub roses, climbers and ramblers at their very best.

# Colour Plates

*Between pp. 96 and 97*

# Introduction

In 1973 my book *Shrub Roses for Every Garden* was published. Its aims were to show that there was a whole world of roses about which many gardeners knew nothing and to help those who had perhaps started on the road to discovery to make the best of what they found. In this it must have succeeded at least to some degree, because in due course all the copies were sold. A reprint was considered, but in the meantime costs had soared, especially those of colour printing, and there was a lot of colour in the book. To reprint it in its original form would have meant a cover price so high that nobody could have afforded to buy it. As Bob Sawyer said in *Pickwick Papers*: 'At the end of a few years you might put all the profits in a wine glass and cover 'em over with a gooseberry leaf.' So what was to be done?

This is the answer, a book with the same aims but with rather less colour, and what there is using photographs from my own collection in place of Marjorie Blamey's specially commissioned paintings. To compensate, the text has been considerably extended – it is about half as long again – and many more varieties are described, including a number of the shrub roses introduced in the last few years and which seem to be proving themselves as stayers. So this is not simply a revised version of the old book. Inevitably some of what I had to say about a number of the roses that appeared before will be much (if not exactly) the same. They have not changed in the meantime, but on the other hand I have learned quite a lot more about many of them and about others, in one or two cases to the extent of at least partially changing my opinion about them. In any form of gardening one of the fascinations is that one never stops finding out new things and one can only write sensibly on any kind of plant in the light of personal experience. If that experience leads to a change of mind it is, admittedly, rather hard on those who have followed the writer's original advice, but at least opinions which were sincerely held at one time but have since been found to have a small leak in them are not perpetuated to mislead others. Fortunately in this case they are very few.

So here it is; what amounts, really, to a new book.

Ever since Canon Reynolds Hole was instrumental in forming what is now the Royal National Rose Society in 1876, which was really the beginning of the widespread use of roses in small gardens as well as large ones, and perhaps even more since, in 1900, the French nurseryman Joseph Pernet-Ducher started the line that led to bright yellow and orange and flame in the garden rose colour range, the popularity of roses has soared. But the concentration has been mainly on bedding roses, the Hybrid Teas and Floribundas. The wonderful old roses were largely forgotten in the stampede to buy the new. Here is my second attempt to redress the balance. And it is to be hoped that a rhubarb leaf will be needed to cover the profits.

## Chapter 1

# The Background

BEFORE making a start, it would be as well to establish what we are talking about, for there has always been confusion and doubt as to what exactly constitutes a shrub rose. In fact there has been confusion and doubt about virtually the whole classification of roses into different families or groups which is, in part at least, the fault of the rose itself. In times gone by, and I am talking now about thousands of years ago, wild or species roses interbred, one kind with another with the greatest enthusiasm, and they gave no thought to the problems they would be causing mankind later on. Nobody was there to record, even on the wall of a cave, the parents of a new rose that might result from such interbreeding.

Much, much later man began to cultivate roses, but it was not until early in the last century that he started to realise that he could do deliberately what the wind and insects had been doing with great industry for centuries – arrange for the deliberate transfer of the pollen of one rose to the flower of another to produce something completely new. The first stage was a dim realisation that this transfer did happen in some way, and so nurserymen planted varieties they wished to cross next to each other and hoped for the best. Sometimes this would appear to have worked, but nobody could really be certain that pollen had not been blown or carried from another rose altogether, planted some distance away. The transfer of pollen by hand was not generally practised until a little over one hundred years ago, and even then proper records of what had been crossed with what were not always kept. If they were, sometimes they were lost, or perhaps were even destroyed by unthinking successors to the original breeders.

The result of all this is that rose ancestry is, with very few exceptions, inextricably mixed up. Botanists have for long been swallowing aspirin after aspirin as they tried to sort it out, and at the end of the 1960s and early in the 1970s, the World Federation of Rose Societies put its collective heads together and decided that something must be done to help the confused gardener, rather than the expert. They were concerned amongst many other things that a term such as shrub roses was far too all-embracing and had no properly defined boundaries, and nobody who has tried to define a shrub rose can quarrel with that.

*The Family Tree of Garden Roses*

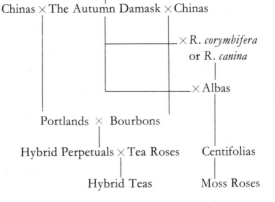

R. *gallica*
|
R. *moschata* × R. *gallica* × R. *phoenicia*
(Musk Rose)
|
Damasks
|
Chinas × The Autumn Damask × Chinas
× R. *corymbifera*
or R. *canina*
× Albas
Portlands × Bourbons
Hybrid Perpetuals × Tea Roses     Centifolias
Hybrid Teas     Moss Roses

Hybrid Chinas × R. *multiflora*
|
Polyantha Pompons × Tea Roses and Hybrid Teas
|
Floribundas

Dates have been omitted deliberately. In some cases they are unknown and in many others very uncertain.

The thought of having to cope with new names for various rose groups may be the equivalent of hitting a lobster-pot when water-skiing to those who have just about managed to master the hitherto basic terms for bedding varieties such as Hybrid Teas and Floribundas, or who have even had a small flirtation with classes in the old rose field. However, it has not been proposed to change by any means everything, and fortunately the area of rose growing with which we are mainly concerned has been changed least of all. As it is unlikely that many new roses will be added to the old groups or that those that do exist will be changed in any way, the old family names such as Gallica, Alba, Centifolia and Bourbon have been retained.

For this reason, and as the new classification is really undergoing a trial period and may well in course of time have to be modified as inconsistencies emerge or new rose families come into existence, I have kept to the traditional ways in this book. The definition of a shrub rose as one that is not normally used for bedding has been applied.

Having established (more or less) our terms of reference, what is it that shrub roses give us that the modern bedding roses cannot? And what have the old ramblers and climbers, which are also covered in this book, to contribute in terms of today? Why bother with them at all? Apart from a very small selection of some of the best, they are not generally stocked by the average nurseryman, and this means that an extra effort may be needed to find them, but it is not really a very big one. Advertisements in the gardening press will soon reveal that there are specialist growers, and together they offer a very wide range indeed. The names of some of them will be found on page 176, so that is one hurdle surmounted without even buying a gardening paper.

With only one exception that I can call to mind, only those roses which are available in current catalogues are discussed in this book, but even if they should vanish from the lists in the future, it does not mean necessarily that they have ceased to exist altogether. A number of wonderful old roses from the past have turned up from time to time 'wasting their sweetness in the desert air' of a neglected garden, and been put back into commerce again once their true identity has been established, often a far from easy task unless accurate colour prints of them exist in old books. Making such discoveries – or even the chance of doing so – is something that has a great appeal to the lover of old roses, but having digressed a little from what I started out to say, I shall now come back to the more straightforward attractions these old roses possess, which cannot be realised by those who have not seen them. On the way I intend to light a fuse under a number of myths and explode them once and for all, such as the one about their unsuitability for small gardens.

Let us start with the beauty and form and the colouring of the flowers. The high-centred bloom with reflexing outer petals of the Hybrid Tea, so much admired nowadays, is not a natural development of the rose. Beautiful as it is, it is entirely a product of cultivation. Practically all the old roses, of the West at any rate, have short centre petals, which result in a more or less cupped bloom in the early stages, often then opening flat or developing into a pompon if the outer petals reflex far enough. It was not until the incorporation of the long-petalled Tea roses from China in the nineteenth century into the breeding lines of Hybrid Perpetuals that the flowers, as a result of careful selection, began to change. This can be seen in the Hybrid Perpetuals themselves even today if one contrasts the blooms of a very early one such as 'Baronne Prévost' of 1842 with those of 'Mrs John Laing' of 1887 or 'Frau Karl Druschki' of fourteen years later, dates which straddle the period during which the Hybrid Tea rose was emerging as a class on its own.

These changes in flower form came about only gradually, the first stage being a very globular bloom in which the centre petals were certainly longer than they had been and, though slow to open out, could not yet really be described as high-centred. A survival of this can be found in the first Hybrid Tea itself, 'La France', but it is hard to say why the new shape should have come to be accepted as the norm. Indirectly, it may have had to do with the coming of the yellow and orange colourings, when people stampeded for the new Pernet varieties. Many of these also had the new flower form and this was accepted as part of the changing picture – a move forward – however mistaken the idea may seem to us now. Also, it was in the latter part of the nineteenth century that rose shows with competitive classes first became popular, and when the organisers were setting their standards for judging it was perhaps natural that the latest types of roses should be chosen as the yardstick and considered the best. Frankly, this is something of a

14

guess, but it seems a reasonable one, and whatever the reason may be it cannot be disputed that, during the last eighty years or so, the older flower forms have come to be considered inferior. Which is, to put it mildly, nonsense.

One has only to consider a very few of the earlier roses as representative of the whole to see the truth of this. Starting with the species, what, for instance, could be more lovely than the infinitely delicate, five-petalled, creamy-yellow single blooms of the Scotch rose R. *spinosissima altaica*, which have the added attraction that they appear before the buds of most other roses even begin to swell? Or the cream stamens at the heart of the light pink single flowers of the Rugosa 'Fru Dagmar Hastrup'? To some people, it is almost an indecency for a rose to show its stamens. Quite why this should be so I do not know, and I rather doubt that they do either. All one can do is to show them something like the amber crown in the centre of the bloom of 'Mermaid', the delicate golden-yellow filaments of R. × *dupontii*, or the maroon stamens which set off the soft pink and yellow blends in the comparatively modern R. *spinosissima* hybrid 'Frühlingsmorgen', and if these and all the others one could name do not convert the unbelievers, clearly nothing will. As a last despairing hope one could try the semi-double, creamy-white clusters of something like R. × *alba semi-plena*, flaunting their yellow stamens as proudly as they deserve.

The blooms of the wine-red Gallica 'Charles de Mills', those of the white Damask 'Madame Hardy', and the blended maroon and violet-purple flowers of the Hybrid Perpetual 'Reine des Violettes' are examples of those absolutely bursting with small petals and which open flat, the petals infolded and quartered in a way not found in any other flower, and in the case of 'Madame Hardy' they surround a small green pointel, an intriguing combination. The petals of the Bourbons 'Madame Pierre Oger' and 'La Reine Victoria' are much larger and fewer in number, curved and shell-like, giving to the blooms a goblet form and a delicacy not found in the huge, cabbagy flowers of their relative 'Madame Isaac Pereire', which have the sumptuous allure of an old-style courtesan. And in complete contrast are the huge corymbs, each of which may well have over a hundred minute white single flowers, which are carried in incredible profusion by a number of the Far Eastern so-called Musk ramblers, or the multi-petalled pompons of 'Little White Pet'. The variations are quite without limit, and

15

one should not forget, either, the blazing scarlet hips that follow the flowers in so many cases, particularly on the wild roses and on the Rugosa family.

Colour we have touched on and it can be said that the old garden and modern shrub roses combined embrace the whole range – always excepting a true blue. This is unlikely ever to come, unless by a freak of nature, as roses lack, except I believe in the leaves of some of them, the essential chemical, delphinidin, which is needed to produce it. The coming of the bright yellow Pernetiana roses has also already been mentioned, and it has produced among the shrub roses examples such as 'Reveil Dijonnais' which would stand out at night in Piccadilly Circus or Times Square. Before that there were Tea roses that did have delicate creamy-yellow tints, but otherwise the old garden roses embraced a wide range of pinks, mauve, lilac, purple and maroon, with crimson being added by 'Slater's Crimson China' in the eighteenth century. Almost without exception, their colours blend well together and mak the most entrancing combinations. On occasions many different tones are found in one bloom and with some of them they change as the flower passes from the half-open bud to a full-blown bloom. The Gallica 'Belle de Crécy' is one that changes slowly from cerise pink to soft parma violet, and the Moss rose 'William Lobb' from soft crimson-purple to violet-grey, both if anything gaining in charm as they do so. And a mention of a Gallica leads one naturally to think of the many striped varieties usually with pink or crimson-maroon striping on a blush-white ground. They abound and there are striped roses in other groups such as the Bourbons, too.

Scent. How often does one hear the words 'Why do modern roses not have as much scent as the old ones?', but you can discover if you dig far enough back that Pliny the Elder in Roman times was saying exactly the same thing. Then, as now, some roses were scented and some were not. A number of the old garden roses we grow today have none at all, but if the majority of them do, and in abundance, this could well be the reason that they have remained in public favour for hundreds of years. The old scentless roses, unless they had outstanding qualities of other kinds, just faded from the reckoning and vanished away. If there is one thing that is certain, however, it is that few roses of any period can match the perfume of 'Madame Isaac Pereire' or the Rugosa 'Roseraie de l'Hay', or that of the so-called Musk ramblers, which has the

16

almost unique quality of floating free in the air so that you do not have to be close to detect it. Almost unique, because it is shared by that comparatively modern rambler 'Albertine' and a few others.

Finally, before we leave the subject, one must not forget the aromatic foliage of the Sweet Briers, or that of R. *primula* where the leaves are extremely decorative as well. In what modern rose can this be found?

Which brings us quite naturally to leaves, and it is here that modern shrub roses and many other varieties of today do come out rather better than many of the old garden roses. On the whole leaves keep their looks considerably longer on the moderns, though disease can strike at both and does. Yet somehow with the old roses it does not seem to have the same dire effects, at least as far as black spot is concerned. It is just that the leaves of groups like the Damasks, Centifolias, Moss roses and several other families look as if they have had enough of it by the end of the summer and are often stained and discoloured. Strategic placing in the garden can make this less noticeable, but this kind of thinking is certainly not needed with the soft grey-green leaves of the Albas or the decorative and long-lasting foliage of species roses such as 'Canary Bird' or R. *rubrifolia*. There is even R. *foliolosa* with narrow leaves resembling those of a willow and roses which give autumn colouring as well, as does R. *virginiana*. It is the Rugosas, however, that must hold pride of place among all the old garden and shrub roses, the brightest of green, with never a sign of ill health.

I have dealt with the misconception about scent, and now come to two others which one hears stated quite dogmatically again and again as fact. Both are equally wide of the truth, and if you pick representative samples from each group described in the pages of the next few chapters and examine them, you are sure to wonder, as I do, how such beliefs came to be widely held. Even, perhaps, how you came to hold them yourself.

Although you can prove them to be untrue simply by reading on, I still think it is worth enlarging a little on them here because they have undoubtedly frightened many people away from shrub roses altogether. They are that all shrub roses only flower once during the course of a year and, as I mentioned earlier, that all of them are too big for a small garden.

Taking them in turn and starting with the statement about them not being remontant, my reaction if this were true would be a simple question: so what? Do we not all grow rhododendrons, lilacs and philadelphus, and do we sit and mope at the thought that their yearly display of bloom will have vanished by early summer? No; we expect this, but the trouble is that the modern remontant rose has led us to think that all roses should behave in the same way. When one gets down to the facts, only the following groups do not flower twice: the wild roses, the Gallicas, the Damasks, the Albas, the Centifolias and Moss roses, and among those that climb, the ramblers and some of the climbers. Even among these there are a few exceptions, but most Chinas, Bourbons, Portlands, Hybrid Perpetuals, Polyanthas, Hybrid Musks and Rugosas either keep going nonstop or put on a fine second showing. And once again there should be a reminder of the hips which in late summer and autumn add a second helping of visual excitement to both remontant and nonremontant kinds.

On the question of size I can be rather briefer, for it is only necessary to say that all except a very few of the wild roses will indeed end up fairly large (though in most cases no bigger than a lilac), but apart from these every other group contains those which could be fitted comfortably into a space 4ft × 3ft (1.2 × 1m). Quite a number will be smaller still.

I hope that all I have said so far has not given the impression that I am extolling old and modern shrub roses at the expense of the more usual bedding roses. I am certainly not, for I grow representatives of just about every group there is, old and new, and I like them all, each in its own way. Or if that statement perhaps indicates a lack of discrimination that I hope I haven't got, I will qualify it by saying most rather than all of them.

There is one way, however, in which the moderns cannot compete. They are not part of history, and in case anyone comes back at me with my own 'so what?', let me try and explain what I mean, even though to some extent I will be attempting to define the indefinable. To me there is something magical in looking each day during the summer months at a rose the Romans knew and loved all of 2,000 years ago; or that the ancient Persians thought so beautiful that they used it to decorate their illuminated manuscripts; or the rose that came from old China to give us our modern repeat-flowering kinds. There is a fascination in growing what may well be the Red Rose of Lancaster or the White Rose of York, or in having a collection that takes one step by step through the line of development of the large flowered bush rose via, in sequence, the Gallicas, the Damasks, the Chinas, the Bourbons and Portlands and finally the Tea roses. Or why not cultivate roses about which a sixteenth-century herbalist could write:

The distilled water of Roses is good for strengthening of the heart, and refreshing of the spirits, and likewise for all things that require gentle cooling.

The same being put in junketting dishes, cakes, sauces and many other pleasant things, giveth a fine and delectable taste.

It mitigateth paine of the eies proceeding from a hot cause, bringeth sleep, which also the fresh roses themselves provoke through their pleasant smell.

Or even this: 'The juyce of these Roses, especially the Damask, doth move to the stoole, and maketh the belly soluble: but most effectuall of all that of the Musk Roses: next to them is the juyce of the Damask, which is more commonly used.'

Then there are the roses in the Empress Josephine's garden at her villa Malmaison, not far from Paris, which were painted by the Belgian artist Redouté. We all know them, for since his time they have been reproduced again and again, as prints and book illustrations, on mats, on wastepaper baskets, on wall plaques and in fact on almost anything one is likely to find about a house that has anything like a flat, or at least smooth, surface. Perhaps we know them too well. They have become, almost, a beautiful cliché, but look again and see how skilfully the artist has combined his eye for composition with (not always infallible) botanical accuracy. They form an unique record of the roses growing in Josephine's time, for she created a collection at Malmaison of every kind and variety then known, and it was she who established a fashion for rose gardens that has lasted to the present day. One can still grow a great many of her roses, though not all the varieties have survived and some that have have had their names changed in the meantime; but to compare the actual blooms of your roses with Redouté's matchless plates is an experience in itself.

However, I am getting carried away. To compare them with the true colours of the Redouté originals as opposed to the sometimes not quite accurate prints, you would have to be almost a millionaire. Sets of his *Les Roses* exchange hands (rarely) for tens of thousands of pounds, but it is possible to see them in a few libraries. Whether the librarians of these would welcome your by then probably rather worse-for-wear and faded rose shedding its petals over the prized folios is another matter, but to me to have some of the roses from the Empress's collection is enough.

As a final thought, consider some of the wonderful names of the old garden roses. 'Robert le Diable', 'Commandant Beaurepaire', 'Rose d'Amour', 'Chapeau de Napoléon', 'Cardinal de Richelieu', 'Comte de Chambord', 'Hebe's Lip', 'Nuits de Young', 'Perle des Panachées', 'La Reine Victoria', 'Tour de Malakoff', 'Prince Camille de Rohan' and 'Reine des Violettes'. I like to lord it over queens, princes, cardinals, comtes and comtesses and commandants in my garden, as socially I would probably only hobnob with 'Du Mâitre d'Ecole'.

*Chapter 2*

# The Species

THESE are the originals that started it all, the five-petalled 'Dog roses' of the world, for to many people any single rose is a Dog rose. Actually R. *canina* – to use its botanical name, which is something we shall have to do when dealing with the species roses – is only one of many. There are thirteen different kinds of wild rose in the United Kingdom alone, and worldwide something around one hundred and fifty, though there is no firm agreement on this last figure. The trouble is that, as we have seen, the wind has been blowing rose pollen about like autumn leaves all over the northern hemisphere (there are no wild roses native to the southern one) for thousands of years, passing it from one rose to another, so that many of them have produced natural hybrids, often with more petals per flower than either of the parents. Or again, extreme variations in growing conditions or climate, even within one country, may gradually over the centuries have brought a change in certain plants of one specific rose, which change becomes in the end firmly set and passed on to succeeding generations. They follow the new pattern, even if moved to a different environment. They are new forms of the original rose, but how is someone discovering one of them for the first time to tell this? It is not easy, and one school of thought takes the view that each variation should be considered as a new species. However, if only because it makes things a great deal easier, I tend to side with the other school. One hundred and fifty or so is enough for anyone to be going on with.

In any case we are concerned here primarily with garden use, and a comparatively small proportion, even of the 150, make a really worthwhile and lasting display. Unless you are a dedicated enthusiast and have space to spare, with many (and this includes all the British wild roses with the possible exceptions of R. *spinosissima* and R. *rubiginosa*) the flowering period, though enchanting while it lasts, is very fleeting. With some, a heavy rainstorm at the peak blooming period could dash the fragile petals to the ground and make it even shorter.

This may sound like a counsel of despair, but it is not. There are plenty of treasures, many from China and other parts of the Far East, from the Middle East, from America and from certain parts of Europe, that more than make up for the lack of flowering stamina in the rest. Some will come into bloom in late spring as herald to the rose season; others flower later. Many are powerfully scented, sometimes in the leaves as well as the petals. A number have the most decorative foliage, either in form or colour or both, with perhaps autumn tints as a bonus. Or there can be a spectacular display of orange or scarlet hips following the flowers from late summer onwards. R. *sericea pteracantha* has decorative thorns, and this particular rose is the only one whose white flowers have four petals. They are some of the earliest to appear.

Garden space is certainly needed for species roses in all but a few cases, for they do grow and grow, and in time some become vast, tangled thickets, reaching perhaps 8ft × 8ft (2.4 × 2.4m). Others, however, though big in overall dimensions, have an open, airy habit, so that their actual size is not so apparent and overwhelming. As they do not cast so much shade, other things can be grown comparatively close to them. An example of the first kind is R. *soulieana*, and of the second, R. *moyesii*. At the other end of the scale, R. *spinosissima* has a vast range of quite small hybrids, known collectively as the Scotch or Burnet roses, many of which grow no more than 3ft (90cm) high. These would appear to be eminently suitable for small areas, and so they are, provided that something can be done to control their spread by suckers. How this can be done will be described in the chapter on Practical Care.

One of the few species roses available from nurseries that does keep on flowering after the first midsummer flush has a name to play anagrams with, R. *fedtschenkoana*. Of considerable attraction, the single white flowers appear on new wood throughout the summer months and the leaves are a pleasing greyish-green.

In the garden, wild roses can be used in a number of ways, but there are one or two points it is worth remembering when making a choice – apart from the question of their size, the single flowering period (which with many nevertheless lasts several weeks), and the fact that it is the minority that bear really showy hips. A number have no great appeal in the second half of the year and the leaves can quite soon lose their fresh brightness. It is not that wild roses are particularly prone to the most common rose diseases of mildew and black spot. On the whole, they are singularly free from them and seem to shrug them off without much effort when they do get them, though someone at the back of the class is sure to put their hand up at this point and say 'What about R. *foetida persiana*? I thought that this was supposed to have spread black spot through all our modern roses when it was used as one parent of the first true yellow garden roses.' This is quite true and when planting it, R. *foetida* itself, and its red and yellow sport R. *foetida bicolor* it is probably a good idea to keep them more or less on their own, but they are exceptions to the general rule.

The point I am making is that some species roses simply become rather tatty-looking late on, and it is as well to avoid these varieties when choosing a rose for specimen planting on its own. The detailed descriptions of varieties which follow this introduction will indicate which species roses are best for this, but all the others can be used with great effect in mixed shrub plantings, where the foliage or flowers of other roses or shrubs will help to disguise the evident late summer weariness of the species, which can be said to be suffering a sort of horticultural hangover from the excesses and delights of the spring.

After the first year or two, species roses may need a little attention from the secateurs if their growth is becoming lopsided, but otherwise it is best to leave them alone, except for cutting out completely any dead wood. There is no particular time of year to do this; all one can say is 'the sooner the better', for dead wood can harbour disease and in any case looks unsightly.

The reasons that one does not do any other pruning are twofold. In the first place, pruning would cut away the long, arching canes which, when laden with flowers along their entire length, give the wild roses their great charm. In the second place, they will flower just as well without it, so why do it? If a wild rose is pruned it will not actually be harmed, but it will lose one of its greatest assets, its informality.

If we do not prune, it does mean that a great deal of thought must be given to planting distances between bushes so that the roses do not have to be cut back drastically simply because not enough room has been left for them to develop properly. Too close planting of shrubs is a trap everyone falls into at one time or another. Though I should know better by this time, I still do it now and again, most notably in recent years (though this was not actually a question of the size of the bush itself) by planting the original, white, single-flowered R. *spinosissima* much too close to a patch of heather. Now, runners from the rose have inextricably mixed the two, and there is nothing I can do about it, short of digging the lot up. Even then, there would probably be pieces of rose root left in the ground, and after a few years I would be back where I started. However, it has served to drive home the importance of thinking ahead. I knew what might happen and ignored it, even though there is a perfectly simple answer to the problem of a rose (or any other plant for that matter) that spreads by underground suckers as freely as the Spinosissimas do. What I should have done, as I have already said, is described in the chapter on Practical Care.

Young plants with feet if not yards of bare earth all round them can look very forlorn for a few years. Nature will, of course, try to fill up the vacant spaces with weeds, but you can beat her to it by putting in spring bulbs, or annuals if you have the time and energy for bedding out. Other plants you can use are violas or the many not-too-rampant campanulas; these will fill the gaps very well until the roses begin to spread themselves. They can then be dispensed with or moved elsewhere.

There are also a number of plants that consort well with wild roses, and not just in their early years. I will go into this more fully later, but briefly here I can say that, without having been asked, foxgloves have seeded themselves amongst a number of mine and look particularly well. The tall spikes of bloom, pushing up through the rose canes, give just the contrast that is needed, both in flower form and habit.

Many of the roses that we are going to be discussing in a moment are not true species, but they are being included in this chapter because they are very close to being so – natural hybrids, or man-made ones between a species and something else that closely resemble a wild rose in the way they grow and flower. Strictly speaking, a rose such as 'Frühlingsgold' should be in the Modern Shrub Roses chapter, because it was raised in 1937. But it is a cross between a wild rose natural hybrid, R. *spinosissima hispida*,

and a Hybrid Tea, 'Joanna Hill', and in every way resembles much
more closely the older side of the family. 'Nevada' of 1927 is
another case in point, and since we are primarily concerned with
the use of these roses in the garden, it seems sensible to keep like
with like.

In this chapter and the ones that follow, dates are given after
each rose name. In the case of species roses, this date shows the
year in which they were introduced to gardeners, for nobody can
say how old they actually are. With cultivated varieties, the date
indicates its year of introduction as a new rose, and is preceded by
the name of the raiser. Where no date and/or raiser's name is given,
it means that these are not known, for records of such things can
be lost and were, in any case, often sketchily kept in the last
century and earlier. It is not unknown, in fact, for a raiser intentionally to give the wrong parentage for one of his roses, so that
rivals cannot follow his pattern of breeding if it looks like being a
successful one, and this can lead to all kinds of confusion.

The parentage (where known) is given after the date and shows
which rose was crossed with which to produce the rose we are
talking about. Dimensions in feet and metres should be treated
with caution and thought of only as an average or an indication.
The size to which one variety of rose will grow can depend on so
many things: the quality of the plant in the first place, and then the
soil, situation and climate in which it is grown, to say nothing of
the care lavished on it in the way of feeding and general cultivation.
Where possible, it is wise to try to see a variety you want fully
established in a garden elsewhere, because this is the only way to
assess not only its size but also its type and habit of growth.
Words (even mine) can never deal with this adequately, just as they
cannot give more than an indication of the beauty and colour of a
flower, or of its scent. Fragrance can vary enormously from one
part of a year and even from one part of a day to another, and the
humidity of the air can affect it.

One other general point. At one time or another in the past, a
number of the old rose varieties were given Latin or botanical
names, which strictly speaking should have been applied to the
original species and not to varieties bred from them and coming to
form a new group on their own. An example of this is the Alba
roses, which were probably derived from a form of R. *corymbifera*
and a Damask. Thus the variety name R. *alba maxima* is incorrect

and should read R. × *alba maxima*, the × being inserted to indicate hybrid origin. Since practically all cultivated roses other than ramblers and climbers, and also excepting the Chinas, Rugosas and miniatures, appear to be descended either directly or indirectly from the Gallicas, and as there is probably an original species R. *gallica*, this is one of the few families which does not have the hybrid sign inserted when a Latin name is used for a variety, e.g. R. *gallica versicolor*, popularly known as 'Rosa Mundi'. In the same way we have R. *chinensis viridiflora* or R. *rugosa alba*, but all the other old rose groups, Damasks, Centifolias, Bourbons and so on come down in a line, though certainly not a straight one, from the wild Gallica and so need the ×. If this sounds confusing all I can say is, read on, and with a bit of luck (and some application) the pattern ought to emerge.

I have taken some care to ensure that, at the time of writing, practically all the species and varieties described in this book can be bought from nurseries, though you will have to go to a specialist in old roses for some of them. But even a specialist cannot hold stocks for ever of a rose for which there is absolutely no demand. It will take up precious space which could be occupied by roses he could sell, and he does have to make a living. So some of the varieties I describe may well vanish from commercial catalogues in time. One can only hope not, and that instead others from the past will be rediscovered and added. This is actually still happening, even though the facts of commercial life are against it, but if it should ever have to cease there is at least one consolation. Most old and many modern shrub roses take quite easily from cuttings. If a variety has vanished from the nursery lists, it may still be possible to find it growing somewhere and to take (always asking permission first) a cutting or cuttings to supply your need. Or it can be budded on to an understock if you know how to do this.

The letters AM, FCC or AGM after a variety description indicate in ascending order Award of Merit, First Class Certificate or Award of Garden Merit from the Royal Horticultural Society. RNRS C OF M and RNRS GM indicate Certificate of Merit or Gold Medal from the Royal National Rose Society. The RHS awards may be given some years after a rose is introduced, which accounts for the apparent discrepancy in dates in some cases. However, the fact that many first-class roses have no award may mean simply that they were never put in competition for one. They may, in fact, be better than some that have them. Plate (Pl.) numbers are given where appropriate.

**R. *californica plena*** 1878, USA. The date given is for R. *californica* itself. That of the semi-double form described here is uncertain, though it must in the nature of things be later. The fragrant, 1½in (3.5cm) flowers have some variation in colouring, from a light lilac-pink to something considerably more intense, with even a touch of crimson in it, and always yellow stamens. Good in dry soils as it is extremely drought resistant, the shrub itself is a graceful grower, the arching canes carrying sprays of bloom all along their length. It will reach 6ft × 5ft (1.8 × 1.5m). Small, neat leaves.

**Canary Bird** This comes from northern China and Korea. Sometimes it is listed as R. *xanthina spontanea*, which is a close relative and may even be one of the parents, the other being R. *hugonis*. About 7ft × 7ft (2.1 × 2.1m) when grown as a bush, but for a smaller space it is quite easy to buy it as a standard, in which form it will not cover much more than 5ft (1.5m) of ground. It may start flowering in April in a good year but will certainly do so in May anywhere short of the Arctic Circle, the blooms lasting three to four weeks with sometimes an odd one or two later at the tips of the shoots. The rounded bush, with attractive, ferny foliage, has each of its long, arching canes literally smothered with 2in (5cm) bright yellow, lightly scented, single flowers, in my garden the first of all to open in spring and all the lovelier for that. Each flower is on a very short stalk arising from a leaf axil, so that they nestle into the leaves. Said to be subject to die-back, but though I have grown it both in standard form and as a bush I have never had this trouble. That it does well in my garden means that it does not mind poor, dry soil. Occasionally a shoot much more vigorous than the rest will come pushing up, and if it gets too long it can look rather odd and out of place. If it is cut back by about a half after flowering, it will then send out arching shoots of its own, forming as it were a second tier to the cake.

**R. × *cantabrigiensis*** (R. × *pteragonis cantabrigiensis*) Hurst, 1931. Another early-flowering yellow, and a better, more vigorous and upright-growing offspring of one that is much better known and more often listed, R. *hugonis*. 7ft × 7ft (2.1 × 2.1m), the arching branches are covered in May and on into June with creamy-yellow, semi-double 2in (5cm) blooms amongst the fern-like leaves. Less graceful in habit than 'Canary Bird' and more compact, it has small round orange hips in late summer, which the latter does not. Hardly any thorns and a sweet fragrance. 'Earldomensis' is a particularly good hybrid. AM 1931.

**Complicata** By no means a species rose and though it certainly does not look it is a Gallica hybrid, perhaps with R. × *macrantha*, a rose of the wild type and of obscure origin. It would appear to have inherited more from the latter than the former, for one would certainly say that 'Complicata' was nearer to a wild than a cultivated variety. It will make a large, mounding shrub of 7ft × 8ft (2.1 × 2.4m), or it loves to scramble up through other shrubs, when it will go considerably higher. It has very large and beautiful single flowers in tremendous profusion, brilliant pink, with a white eye and yellow stamens. They are often described as being as large as saucers, but if so they are ones which would go with coffee cups rather than teacups. They certainly are big, however, and appear all along the arching shoots, set off well by the mid-green, semi-glossy, very pointed leaves. In full bloom a sight not to be forgotten. AM 1951, FCC 1958. See Pl. 4.

**R. × *dupontii*** Some time earlier than 1817, and possibly raised in the Empress Josephine's garden at Malmaison, a cross between a Gallica hybrid and the Musk Rose. Named after André Dupont, Director of the Luxembourg Gardens in Paris. It will build up to a 7ft × 7ft (2.1 × 2.1m) bush, coming into bloom at midsummer. The flowers, in clusters of four or five, are up to 3in (8cm) across and have very wide, rounded petals which overlap, so that at first glance they seem semi-double. Creamy-white and with odd petals flushed blush-pink, they have a rich musk fragrance, which is to be expected with a Musk rose on one side of the family. Golden stamens of great delicacy are an added attraction. It can be grown as a free, lax bush or as a pillar rose to about 8ft (2.4m). Good tolerance of rain and a long flowering period.

**R. *ecae*** From Afghanistan in 1880, though for some reason early writers, including Gertrude Jekyll, decided that it had come from

28

Abyssinia. This is a species for a small garden as it will not often go over about 5ft (1.5m) or spread out to more than 4ft (1.2m). Starting to appear in late spring, its bright yellow, 1in (2.5cm) single flowers have the intense colour of a buttercup and are borne on wiry reddish-brown canes. The leaves are small and dainty. AM 1933.

***R. fedtschenkoana*** Introduced in 1890 from Turkestan, and almost unique among the species in that it continues to produce its 2in (5cm) white, single flowers with prominent yellow stamens on short side shoots from the main canes and their laterals right through the summer. Occasional flowers have a pink flush, but though they come quite freely at no time is this what one could term a spectacular rose. It is, however, a very pleasing one in a gentle kind of way, with the blooms set off by pale, grey-green leaves, while in the second half of the summer there will be red hips in addition. Reasonably upright to about 8ft (2.4m), it will cover about 6ft (1.8m) of ground and so does need space to be seen at its best. Because of its attractive leaves, it can make a pleasing addition to a general shrub planting. The bristly, dark wood is armed with many straight thorns.

***R. farreri persetosa*** From northwest China and introduced in 1914. A dainty, very twiggy, mounding shrub which will reach 4–5ft (1.2–1.5m) and about the same across. Tiny leaves with up to nine leaflets, sometimes tinted bronze-purple, form the background for the multitudes of pink single flowers of a size (about ¾in or 19mm) which has given it the popular name of the Three-penny Bit Rose, possibly a source of puzzlement to the younger generation of gardeners. It was R. *farreri* itself that was introduced by Farrer in 1915, from which the form *persetosa*, with rather deeper pink flowers, was selected by E.A. Bowles and is now the one generally available. Small, coral-red hips.

***R. foetida*** and ***R. foetida bicolor*** These can be taken together since they are identical except in the colour of their flowers. In R. *foetida* they are about the most brilliant yellow of any wild rose, and in R. *foetida bicolor* the yellow is retained on the face of the petals but the reverse is a flaming orange-red. The latter rose is a sport of the former and the pair are sometimes known as 'Austrian

29

Yellow' and 'Austrian Copper'. Why this is so one can only surmise, but the most likely reason would seem to be that cultivation in Austria was an early chapter in the story of their move westwards from their original home in Asia Minor and the Middle East. Probably there was a halt in Austria and then, after a time, they were 'rediscovered', and on moving onwards once more to France and England and eventually to America, the name of their adopted home was given to them in error. Much the same thing happened when early China roses were rested at the Calcutta Botanic Gardens on their way to the West and found that all of a sudden they had become Bengal roses.

Both roses make as a rule not particularly vigorous and rather spindly 5ft × 4ft (1.5 × 1.2m) shrubs, the 1¼in (3cm) single flowers coming on short stems on the old wood and frequently on the ends of the branches. They have a peculiar, heavy scent which has given them the family name, though it certainly cannot be described as fetid. Best grown with the protection of a wall, when they will flower freely provided there is plenty of sun as well, though rather strangely considering their country of origin they seem to do better in cooler districts and need deep, rich soil to give of their best. Slow to establish, they resent any but the lightest of pruning. Occasionally the odd branch of R. *foetida bicolor* will sport back to its yellow parent. The one real problem with both these roses is black spot, but despite this drawback they are exciting to have around. Prior to 1590.

**R. foetida persiana**  This could really be bracketed with the last two since it is another sport of R. *foetida*, in this case dating from 1837. It has a second name, the Persian Yellow, which is more logical than the popular one given to its relatives because it does come from Persia, but I think that it justifies being separated because it has a distinction that is all its own. The very double yellow flowers were the ones used by Joseph Pernet-Ducher, the French nurseryman from Lyon referred to earlier, to produce the first true yellow garden roses when he crossed them with various Hybrid Perpetuals and Teas and was able to put 'Rayon d'Or' on the market in 1910. It is to his work we ascribe the yellow, orange and flame-coloured roses in our gardens – except for a few wild ones – although the susceptibility of the *foetidas* to black spot was passed on to the other roses as well as their colour. Black spot was known, but does not appear to have been a serious problem before their day. In habit and cultural requirements the Persian Rose is much the same as the others, if perhaps a little less vigorous and with the double flowers a little less fond of rain. See Pl. 1.

**R. forrestiana** From western China. Eventually this will form a very large shrub up to 7ft (2.1m) tall, but it takes its time and will remain quite small for a number of years. The canes are long and arching and bear at midsummer smallish single carmine-pink flowers which have a white eye and pale yellow stamens. They come in clusters on short stalks, surrounded by the most unusual leafy bracts. These in due course frame the small, bright red hips that follow. The plum-red new wood is another attraction. Not a showy shrub, but an interesting one. AM 1956.

**R. × harisonii** ('Harison's Yellow') Raised in New York about 1830. Said to have been taken west by the American pioneers and to have become naturalised along many of the old wagon trails, this rose has such good qualities that it also went very rapidly in the other direction across the Atlantic, though not in order to mark the shipping routes. Shining yellow, rather informal double flowers set off by bright green leaves appear very early in the year on a tough and vigorous bush which is apt to branch in unexpected directions. This can cause it to look unbalanced, so it is probably best to grow it along with other shrubs rather than use it as a specimen, though it does not resent a certain amount of pruning to keep it in shape and is not a rose that is spoiled in appearance by this. Its general cheerfulness will light up any garden in spring and the flowers have a strong, heavy scent which links it to R. *foetida persiana*, one of its parents, the other probably being R. *spinosissima*. Golden stamens distinguish it from another R. *spinosissima* hybrid, the very similar 'Williams' Double Yellow', in which their place is taken by green carpels.

**R. hugonis** 'Headleyensis' About 1920. R. *hugonis* × R. *spinosissima altaica*. Like R. × *cantabrigiensis*, this is another more beautiful and even larger (9ft × 12ft) (2.7m × 3.7m) seedling form of the early-flowering single yellow R. *hugonis*. It is very fragrant and the medium-sized flowers are of soft creamy-yellow, carried all along the widely sweeping, delicate branches. They are not unlike large wild primroses. Very much for big gardens only, where the sight of a bush in full bloom in late spring is something that, once seen, will not be forgotten.

***R. × macrantha* hort.**  Before 1823. This one is a bit of a puzzle, and though nobody knows its origin, it is fairly certain that it is not a true wild rose. That is what the 'hort.' after its name means, short, of course, for horticultural. It is one of the sprawlers or, more kindly, a trailing rose. Only about 5ft (1.5m) high, it will reach out in all directions to 9–10ft (2.7–3m), with its lax canes studded with 4in (10cm) single, blush-pink or almost white flowers with golden stamens. They come in small clusters, have a sweet scent and are followed by ¾in (2cm) round red hips. Use it for making a low foreground to a shrub planting or for running wild over banks. It has given rise to some interesting hybrids, one of which appears below and the other, 'Raubritter', under Modern Shrub Roses.

***R. × macrantha* 'Lady Curzon'**  A 1901 hybrid with a Rugosa that does not much resemble either parent, it forms a great 8ft × 8ft (2.4 × 2.4m), rounded, tangled bush which will scramble up into a neighbouring tree or tall shrub if given the chance. The flowering period at midsummer is rather short, but spectacular while it lasts, the whole rose being covered, and I do mean covered, with the most marvellous single, pink, 4in (10cm) flowers with creamy stamens and curiously wrinkled petals. 'Daisy Hill', blush pink, is another good Macrantha hybrid.

***R. moyesii***  First introduced from western China in 1894, but made no particular impact until reintroduced in 1903. William Robinson must then have helped, for writing in a late edition of his *The English Flower Garden* he said: 'Men talk of getting fine things by crossing this, but they will never get anything so good.' Well, he was not quite right if the parentage of that unbeatable rose 'Nevada' is what the reference books say it is and the doubters are wrong, for R. *moyesii*, or at least one form of it, is given as a parent. But all the same, Robinson had justification for saying what he did because the new rose he was looking at really is something. It will grow up to 12ft (3.7m) in height and 10ft (3m) across, but is not too dense in habit, so that it is a good companion for plants that like partial shade. It comes into flower in late spring and keeps going for many weeks, during which it is a mass of brilliant crimson-red, single 2½–3in (6–7.5cm) flowers with creamy stamens setting them off to perfection, one or two blooms on each short spur along the gently arching branches. It has small, bluish-green leaves but little if any scent. From late summer onwards there are the most striking bottle-shaped hips, hanging in clusters and each fully 2in (5cm) long. AM 1908, FCC 1916, AGM 1925.

*R. moyesii* 'Eos' Ruys, 1950. R. *moyesii* × 'Magnifica'. This hybrid has semi-double blooms of a vivid coral-red but not the usual hips of the family. About 12ft × 7ft (3.7 × 2.1m), the canes are also coral-red when young but are of a much softer tone than the flowers.

*R. moyesii* 'Geranium' Raised at the Wisley Gardens of the Royal Horticultural Society in 1938, this is the best of the family where space is a consideration, though it is still hardly a 'wee sleekit cowering beastie'. The blooms are of a slightly lighter red than R. *moyesii* itself though not lacking in vividness, and are very striking with their cream stamens. At 10ft × 8ft (3 × 2.4m) only relatively compact in comparison with its parent, but it has rather more foliage and the hips are, if anything, bigger. See Pl. 2.

*R. moyesii* 'Highdownensis' Hillier, 1928. Another big one, 10ft (3m) in height and as much across. The small, dainty leaves of the type are rather glaucous on the undersides and the arching stems are a rich, reddish brown. The deep pink blooms are 2½in (6cm) across, single, and have buff anthers. Large, brilliant scarlet hips, carrying on the family tradition of a fondness for the bottle. AM 1928. See Pl. 2.

*R. moyesii* 'Marguerite Hilling' Hilling, 1959. A deep pink sport of 'Nevada' and similar in every way except for the colouring. AM 1960.

*R. moyesii* 'Nevada' Dot, 1927. 'La Giralda' × R. *moyesii*. As I indicated above, there is doubt about the parentage given here. 'La Giralda' was a pink large flowered Hybrid Tea from the same raiser, but if the other parent was R. *moyesii* itself there ought not

33

to be any second blooming with 'Nevada'. This hardly ever happens with the initial cross of a once-flowering rose, so at least a second or third generation Moyesii hybrid must have been involved. But to look to the present rather than the past, this is one of the most magnificent of all garden shrubs and not just the most magnificent of roses that resemble species. It is also one of the large ones, growing 7ft × 7ft (2.1 × 2.1m) or more as a fairly dense, arching bush. The reddish-brown stems have few thorns and the foliage, although on the small side, is abundant and much more rounded than that of most roses. Black spot is not unknown, but I have never seen it as a serious problem. The real glory is in the flowers, which are semi-double, about 3½in (9cm) across, and of a very pale creamy-white, occasionally slightly flushed with pink, though this can become much more pronounced in hot weather. They appear on the short side shoots from the old wood and also in clusters on the ends of growth of the current year, and in such profusion that the whole bush is almost completely hidden by them, for they actually overlap each other. The main flush is in early summer and the bush will then bloom intermittently until the second rather less prolific flowering in early autumn. Very little scent and few hips. AM 1949, FCC 1954. See Pl. 2.

**R. multibracteata** From western China, 1910. This makes a huge, very prickly shrub with tiny greyish-green leaves which are scented like the Sweet Brier (for which see under R. *rubiginosa*). The 1in (2.5cm) single, rosy-lilac flowers are scented and are borne in corymbs all over the bush for several weeks from late midsummer. Each of the long shoots terminates in a many-flowered cluster, and there are numerous, leafy bracts which give this rose its name. Small, hairy hips follow. It appears in the ancestry of 'Queen Elizabeth'.

**R. ×paulii rosea** Prior to 1903. Sport of R. ×*paulii*. A low-growing but widely spreading rose that will smother weeds as though a blanket had been thrown over them, though it will take four or five years to achieve its full effectiveness in this. No more than 4ft (1.2m) high, the long, wickedly thorny canes will spread out to a diameter of 12–15ft (3.7–4.5m) and occasionally a tip that has touched the ground will root and take it even further. The flowers are large, single and of a soft pink, not unlike those of a

34

clematis, richly scented and with pale yellow stamens; they come
with the greatest of freedom all along the gently arching canes.
The leaves show strong influence of the Rugosa parent. In its early
years, before the canes have mounded one over the other to make a
screen dense enough to keep the light from the soil below, the
thorny canes may make weeding between them both hazardous
and painful, but it is worth persisting. R. × *paulii* itself is similar
but white. See Pl. 2.

**R. pomifera duplex**  A chance garden hybrid of R. *pomifera*, but
with semi-double flowers. It is the best of the two for the garden
from the point of view of flower display, though it will probably
have rather fewer of the large, rounded, russet-red hips which,
though they have given this rose an alternative popular name of
the Apple Rose, to me much more resemble very large goose-
berries. Soft green, downy foliage and pink blooms coming from
carmine buds. The garden form is also known as Wolley-Dod's
Rose, after the Rev. Wolley-Dod, in whose garden it was first
noted. See Pl. 2, showing the hips of the single form.

**R. rubiginosa**  Botanically, this should be R. *eglanteria*, which,
being the first of the two names given to it, should take precedence.
But usage seems to favour R. *rubiginosa*, and there are the alternative
names of Sweet Brier and Eglantine at the more popular level.
Probably not a first choice for any but the wild garden, for its
single pink flowers are fleeting and it will make a huge tangle of
canes which will be difficult to control. However, it does have an
unusual feature in that the foliage is strongly aromatic and the
scent will waft in the early summer air for yards around on a damp
evening. I would say its chief distinction is as the dominant parent
in the crosses that produced the Penzance Briers, which were
raised by Lord Penzance at the end of the last century. Their
flowers are better, they are not all quite so unruly in the way they
grow, and the scented foliage has sometimes been passed on in the
breeding line. There are quite a large number of them altogether.
Here are four of the best:

**R. rubiginosa 'Amy Robsart'**  1894. Rich pink flowers, semi-
double, in early summer and scarlet hips in the autumn. 8ft × 8ft
(2.4 × 2.4m). AM 1853.

**R. rubiginosa 'Lady Penzance'** 1894. Possibly the best blooms of all the Penzance roses, and only making a shrub 6ft × 6ft (1.8 × 1.8m). The single, yellowish-copper flowers in early summer reflect the other parent, R. *foetida*, which also means that black spot is likely, but then this is true of the group in general.

**R. rubiginosa 'Lord Penzance'** 1894. More robust generally than 'Lady Penzance', though it does not grow much taller. The scented single flowers are of a fawny-yellow. FCC 1890.

**R. rubiginosa 'Meg Merrilees'** 1894. As large as 'Amy Robsart', but with crimson, single, scented flowers.

**R. rubrifolia** From the mountains of central and eastern Europe prior to 1830. This makes a fairly large 6ft × 6ft (1.8 × 1.8m) bush, open in habit and with few thorns on the new wood, though they mysteriously materialise later on the old. The very small pink flowers come in clusters of seven or eight but are not showy. Round, bright red hips follow them and make a considerable impact. However, it is the colouring of the rest of the bush that makes it really well worth growing. The long, thin, arching canes have distinctive reddish-brown bark and the pointed leaves are a most unusual grey-green with a purple, plum-like sheen which is intensified if the bush is in light shade. Not under a tree, of course, which will make any rose spindly, but perhaps against a north wall. AM (for fruit) 1949. See Pl. 2.

**R. sericea pteracantha** (R. *omeiensis pteracantha*) From southwestern China in 1890. Very early into flower, about the same time as 'Canary Bird', the single rather fleeting blooms have four petals instead of the usual five, which is distinction enough to be going on with. But there is more to come. It forms a very vigorous, almost impenetrable shrub, often as much as 10ft × 10ft (3 × 3m), the wide-spreading branches bearing huge thorns, flattened and enlarged at the base and continuing along the canes in almost unbroken lines, like the armour on some prehistoric monster. On the young growth these are of a translucent red and are extremely striking with the sun behind them because it makes them glow. When mature they lose this brilliance and become both hard and sharp. It would not be wise to learn your pruning on this rose, but

36

it is one species that does benefit from cutting back fairly hard if you want plenty of the new and very decorative shoots for flower arrangements.

**R. soulieana** Yet another from western China, this time about 1837, and another large bush, certainly 10ft × 10ft (3 × 3m) when fully grown. Of arching, rather sprawling habit, though mounding itself up until it forms a dense thicket. The small leaves are an attractive grey-green and set off to perfection the hundreds of single white flowers that open from yellow buds and have a yellow centre and stamens. In large clusters, they have a sweet scent. Orange-red hips follow them.

**R. spinosissima** This is the original, short-growing, spiny (hence the Latin name) single white rose of the wild coastal regions of Europe and elsewhere. Unlikely to top 3ft (1m), it forms a dense twiggy cover to the ground, spreading with incredible rapidity by underground suckers. The flowers come very early in the year and are followed by round, maroon-black hips. Useful for a piece of dry, sandy waste ground, where it will thrive, but principally of note as the progenitor of a vast number of seedlings of even greater beauty and general usefulness. Collectively they are known as the Scotch or Burnet roses, in the first place because some of the early hybrids were raised in Scotland, and in the second because the small leaves, each with many leaflets, were thought to resemble the herb burnet. Some of the other small ones are 'Double Yellow', 'Double White', *bicolor* (see Pl. 3) and 'William III' (magenta), all of which are fairly typical of the family. There are, however, a number of much larger roses in the group. Here are a few of them:

**R. spinosissima altaica** (R. *altaica*, R. *grandiflora*, R. *sibirica*) From the Altai Mountains in Siberia. One of the least prickly of this family and also one of the most lovely. In spring of each year the 7ft (2.1m) arching canes bear along their entire length single, creamy-white flowers with golden stamens. These are followed by clusters of striking and very dark, shiny, maroon-purple hips which, unless looked at closely, appear black. I would put this rose on a par with 'Canary Bird' as a herald of the rose season. Its flowers are considerably larger, though their season is shorter, and possibly the leaves, large for a Spinosissima, are not as decorative

37

as those of the other rose for the remainder of the summer. They are grey-green and the stems dark brown.

**R. spinosissima 'Frühlingsanfang'**   Kordes, 1950. 'Joanna Hill' × R. *spinosissima altaica*. This is one of the famous Frühlings group of roses produced by the well-known German breeder, using various forms of the Burnet rose as one parent. Part of his aim was to produce winter-hardy roses that would withstand the cold of northern Europe. 'Frühlingsanfang' has large, single, ivory-white flowers in early summer which grow all along the arching branches and are very fragrant. They are followed by maroon-red hips amongst the dark green foliage, which takes on autumn tints as it ages. Up to 8ft × 8ft (2.4 × 2.4m).

**R. spinosissima 'Frühlingsduft'**   Kordes, 1949. 'Joanna Hill' × R. *spinosissima altaica*. Of particular interest in contrast to 'Frühlingsanfang', in that it has exactly the same parents. Here the offspring has not taken after the species rose, at least as far as the flowers are concerned. 'Joanna Hill' is a Hybrid Tea and the blooms take after it in form, with scrolled, high-centred buds. They are creamy-apricot, double of course, and richly scented. The bush, once-flowering at midsummer, will reach 6ft × 6ft (1.8 × 1.8m).

**R. spinosissima 'Frühlingsgold'**   Kordes, 1937. 'Joanna Hill' × R. *spinosissima hispida*. Occasionally listed under the translation of its name, 'Spring Gold', this makes an enormously vigorous shrub, quickly reaching 8–9ft (2.4–2.7m) with its long branches arching outwards as though there were a ten-pound salmon on the end of every one. In fact, each one is laden in early summer with enormous 4–5in (10–13cm) creamy-yellow, semi-double flowers, opening wide but in which some of the petals curve inwards. The stamens are amber and the scent is glorious. The rather pointed, medium-green leaves seem to be nearly disease-proof. In every respect a great rose, fully deserving its AM 1950, FCC 1955 and AGM 1965. See Pl. 11.

**R. spinosissima 'Frühlingsmorgen'**   Kordes, 1942. ('E.G. Hill' × 'Cathrine Kordes') × R. *spinosissima altaica*. The only one of this particular group of roses that is to some extent remontant,

38

though the second crop of flowers will not be a match for the first. The 4in (10cm) single blooms must be counted as among the most beautiful of any rose, a soft pink shading to the palest of yellow in the centre, where there are maroon stamens. There can be some fade after a while, but there is no loss of beauty. Not such a strong grower as 'Frühlingsgold', it is also more bushy, reaching about 6ft × 5ft (1.8 × 1.5m) with quite small, matt, medium-green leaves. Strong fragrance. AM 1951. See Pl. 3.

**R. spinosissima 'Ormiston Roy'** Doorenbos, 1953. R. *spinosissima* × R. *xanthina*. A 4ft (1.2m) bushy shrub, sturdy and flowering early, and ideal for a small garden. It has single, deep yellow flowers, the petals veined darker, and with blackish-maroon hips to follow.

**R. spinosissima 'Stanwell Perpetual'** Lee, 1838. R. × *damascena semperflorens* × R. *spinosissima*. When I said just now that 'Frühlingsmorgen' was the only one of its group to be remontant, I was referring to the Frühlings family and not the Spinosissimas in general. However, I might almost have been, for 'Stanwell Perpetual' is, I believe, the only other exception. It forms a rather lax and possibly even straggly bush which would need some support to achieve perhaps 6ft (1.8m), though if two or three are planted as a group they can help to hold each other up. It is very thorny and has small, greyish-green foliage. Flowering first in early summer, it is then seldom without bloom until the autumn, though there is no second big display. About 3in (7.5cm) across, the blooms are very double and open flat with quilled petals, white flushed pink at first, fading almost to pure white. Little fragrance despite its Damask connections, and not a lover of rain. A very lovely rose, however, when the sun shines on it, and new flowers will soon replace any that suffer from the weather. See Pl. 3.

**R. virginiana** (R. *lucida*, R. *humilis*) From America some time before 1807, this makes a spreading, informal shrub, the arching canes with their hooked thorns reaching perhaps 6ft × 5ft (1.8 × 1.5m). It may reach out even further in time by suckering, which makes this a plant for the (intentionally) wild garden. The single, cerise-pink flowers do not appear until well into the summer and are

39

followed by small red hips. The glossy leaves give an added splash of colour in the autumn.

R. *virginiana alba* is a white-flowered form, possibly a hybrid with R. *carolina*. There is also an extremely beautiful double form known as 'Rose d'Amour' or the 'St Mark's Rose', almost certainly a hybrid as well and perhaps a little more compact than the true species. The scented flowers here are pink and rather deeper in the centre. This is probably the best garden form and, like the parent, it blooms late.

**R. webbiana** From the Himalayas, Afghanistan and Turkestan, 1879. Very early into bloom, this makes a graceful, arching, 6ft × 6ft (1.8 × 1.8m) shrub which is very nearly thornless. The grey-green leaves are fern-like in their delicacy and form an appropriate background for the masses of 1½–2in (4–5cm) single, pale pink blooms which are carried at the terminals of the main and side shoots in clusters of five or six. They have a sweet fragrance. Small, scarlet, bottle-shaped hips follow. AM 1955.

*Chapter 3*
# The Gallicas

THIS is the oldest family of cultivated roses, with written records in a few cases going back at least to the sixteenth century. Since these records are not catalogues of sixteenth-century rose nurseries announcing new introductions, the Gallicas are clearly much older than that: the rose depicted in colour in a wall painting in the Minoan palace of Knossos on Crete is thought to be one of them. Or a rose from Abyssinia known to the Romans as R. *sancta* was probably another. It should be said, however, that most of the varieties we grow nowadays are hybrids of comparatively recent origin, recent, that is, in terms of the total span of rose history.

Though coming from parts of southern Europe and western Asia, the actual name Gallica and the alternatives of French Rose or Rose of Provins are tokens of a long association with France. The town of Provins, southeast of Paris, was the centre of an area where the oldest Gallica variety we know, 'Officinalis', was grown in vast quantities from the Middle Ages onwards, both for the preparation of a wide range of herbal remedies for every disease imaginable (so that it was also known as The Apothecary's Rose) and for the making of conserves from the deep pink petals. One must be careful, however, not to confuse this, the Provins Rose, with the Rose of Provence, which is the Centifolia and again largely developed in a country other than France, in this case the Netherlands.

It is dangerous to generalise about any group of roses, but one can say with reasonable confidence that the majority of Gallicas make compact bushes, not usually more than 3–4ft (1–1.2m) high, so that they will fit very well into the small garden or a small space in a large one. They are fine for planting in the foreground of a shrubbery and three or four on their own will give a good splash of colour, though at midsummer only. They can be used for low

41

hedges dividing one part of a garden from another or for lining a path or drive, but here caution is needed. They are not roses that produce showy hips, and towards the end of the summer the leaves, inclined to be on the rough side anyway, can look extremely scruffy and are by no means proof against mildew. If you have plenty of space for a Gallica hedge, fine, and nothing will put on a gayer show when it is in flower, but it should not be in a place where it will dominate your garden for the rest of the year. There are many other roses, some of them remontant, which will do just as well, so if in doubt keep your Gallicas for a mixed planting where they can retire quietly once the excitement of their mid-summer performance is over.

Wherever they are planted, they will spread quite freely by suckering if they are on their own roots, which can be quite an advantage for thickening a hedge but a considerable nuisance elsewhere. Use the runners to increase your stock by cutting away those with roots and planting them in a nursery bed for the first year.

Many of the Gallicas have almost thornless stems, but they do have prickles and bristles instead, which can be rubbed off with your finger if you have nothing better to do with your time. The leaves are, as I have said, rough to the touch, ranging from dark to medium green. The flower buds are distinctively rounded and the blooms are held aloft above the plants on thin but firm stalks. The colour range includes pinks, mauves, purples and maroons, and some that combine two or more of these together, the intensity of the colours varying considerably in different soils and situations. Striped sports such as 'Rosa Mundi' and 'Perle des Panachées' are quite common and are some of the gayest of the old garden roses.

Most soils suit Gallicas, which are tough and hardy. With the more bushy growers no real pruning is necessary because they send up new growth without its help, but considerable thinning out of the more twiggy kinds after flowering will keep the bushes from becoming too tangled and make them healthier by letting in air. For hedges, a gentle clipping over in winter with garden shears will help to keep them tidy, but the emphasis must be on gentle. Follow their natural outlines as far as possible. Topiary is not for Gallicas – or for any other rose for that matter.

As we shall see, one or two Gallicas depart markedly from the family characteristics I have outlined above. 'Complicata' (described in the Species chapter) and 'Scarlet Fire' are varieties that make vigorous, rambling shrubs, the flowers of which are either single or semi-double, so that they are in every way untypical, even if delightfully so. Others such as 'Cardinal de Richelieu' and 'Empress Josephine' are fairly lax and spreading, though not very large overall. Rose families, like human ones, have rebels and those who do not wish to conform.


**Alain Blanchard** Vibert, 1839. Probably a Centifolia × a Gallica. This forms a 5ft × 3ft (1.5 × 1m) rather lax bush with mid-green, roughish leaves and, exceptionally for a Gallica, it is very thorny. The flowers, however, more than make up. Medium-sized, cupped and almost single, they have crimson-scarlet petals surrounding golden stamens, the crimson soon becoming mottled with maroon. Perhaps this sounds odd, but it looks just right.

**Anaïs Segales** 1837. Despite what I said about the family in general, here is the second of our Gallicas with thorns, but blame the alphabetical order for that. Where they come from in this case we do not know, but this rose makes a small, freely branching bush with light green leaves which reaches about 3ft × 3ft (1 × 1m). The very double flowers are light rose-pink, deepening towards the centre where there is a green pointel. They open flat, with neatly arranged, infolded petals.

**Belle de Crécy** Roesser, 1848 or earlier. Here at last is our first nearly thornless Gallica. Lax, arching branches covered in matt, lead-green leaves bear flowers at midsummer in the greatest profusion, among the most beautiful of all. They are very fragrant and open a rich, purplish pink, which quickly changes to wonderful blends of lilac, purple, slate-grey and soft pink. Clearly a rose with champagne in its veins rather than sap, for the profusion of bloom is quite outstanding, especially in a hot, dry summer. I have seen it said that a late frost will distort some of the flowers, but even in my somewhat cold garden this has never happened. Some other shrubs to lean on will help to show this rose to its best advantage.

**Belle Isis** Parmentier, 1845. If Gallicas in general can be said to suit a small garden, this will suit one that is truly miniscule, for it will probably not exceed 3ft × 3ft (1 × 1m) and makes a neat and extremely attractive small bush. There are two things about it that are not typical of the Gallicas: it is the only one to have flesh-pink tones in its fully double, fragrant flowers, and it is another of those with thorny stems, inherited from an unspecified rose family of the past. It flowers for a long period at midsummer and a distinctive feature is the markedly toothed leaves. This was the rose which, crossed with the Floribunda 'Dainty Maid', produced the marvellous modern shrub rose 'Constance Spry'.

**Camaieux** 1830. Not the most robust of growers, this will reach about 4ft × 2ft (1.2m × 60cm) only on the best of soil and with careful cultivation on anything less than the best. The effort is well worthwhile, however, for the flowers are sensational. The opening blooms are soft pink, striped and splashed with carmine-purple, the colours merging after the first day, though in hot, sunny weather the stripes fade to purple or grey with a white background before they do so. Finally the loosely arranged petals become a soft, uniform, lilac-grey; but whatever the colour blending, and you can have all stages on the bush at the same time, it is always very pleasing to the eye. There is a rich fragrance, too.

**Cardinal de Richelieu** 1840. Smooth leaves for a change on this striking Gallica that has 3in (7.5cm), sumptuous, very double flowers of a dusky maroon-purple which reflex their petals on opening to reveal a white eye. They come in small clusters, heavy enough to weigh down the laxer canes, and can start to look untidy after a while as they fade to a dusty purple. The early colouring is particularly rich, however, though not quite the glowing red of a cardinal's robe. The wood of the canes is shiny and dark green, dulling on maturity, and there are few thorns. Not at its best on poor, dry soils, in which it will need extra attention.

**Charles de Mills** A vigorous and free-blooming bush, reaching a compact 4ft × 4ft (1.2 × 1.2m). Its flowers are unique. The opening buds have been well described as resembling small, sliced-off beetroot, an apt description which gives no hint of the beauties to come. In fact the beetroot stage is the second, for the first hint of colour one sees is pale pink. Logically, pale pink flowers should follow; but no. They open into blends of plum-crimson, purple

44

and maroon of the greatest richness, crammed with petals, cup-shaped at first but flat or slightly reflexed later, holding their form until the petals drop. The support of a stake is advised because the flowers are very large for this family and can weigh down the rather slender canes. See Pl. 4.

**Duc de Guiche** Prévost, 1829. Perfectly formed flowers, cupped at first and opening flat in rich crimson, becoming veined and flushed with purple. They are scented and filled with petals neatly infolded and often quartered in the best old rose style. Some reflexing of the outer petals comes in time and occasionally a green eye shows of the kind to be found in the better-known Damask rose 'Madame Hardy'. It makes a bushy shrub about 4ft × 4ft (1.2 × 1.2m) with, in a family not noted for them, attractive, mid-green leaves. It likes a cool climate and can look a bit sorry for itself in a hot, dry summer.

**Duchesse de Buccleugh** 1846. One of the last of the Gallicas to come into bloom, some three to four weeks after the others, but in late midsummer it more than makes up for the wait and, of course, lengthens the flowering season of the group as a whole. Large, very double and opening flat and quartered, the flowers are crimson-pink fading to a lighter colour at the petal edges. The shrub is bushy with good leaves and will reach about 5ft × 5ft (1.5 × 1.5m).

**Du Maître d'Ecole** Age unknown and also, unfortunately, the reason for this rose's strange name, though it has been said rather vaguely that it was named after the schoolmaster who raised it. This does seem, however, to be a glimpse of the obvious. Perhaps we will never know now, but he must have been proud of his rose with its very large (up to 4in or 10cm), double, quartered flowers, freely borne and a deep rose-pink, veined purple and fading to lilac-pink. Flat at first, the petals reflex after a time, and the weight of the blooms when in full spate will arch out the canes of the 3ft (1m) bush to a diameter of something like 4ft (1.2m). There is likely to be some fading as the flowers age, but earlier the reddish buds, with their long, feathery calyces, are an attraction in themselves.

**Empress Josephine** Also goes under the name of 'Francofurtana' or R. × *francofurtana*. Sometimes said to have been named after the Empress when she grew it at Malmaison but, though it has been known since before her time, it was not named until after her death. It is a fairly lax bush, 4ft × 4ft (1.2 × 1.2m) though occasionally rather more, well branched, tough and reliable. The flowers are not as strongly scented as most others in this group but otherwise lack for nothing, being large and moderately full, if rather loosely formed, and with waved petals. Of a clear, deep rose-pink with a hint of purple, they are veined and shaded a lighter pink. Large hips appear in late summer but are not particularly showy. See Pl. 4.

**Georges Vibert** Robert, 1853. The comparatively small flowers are freely produced on a compact, upright bush of 4ft × 3ft (1.2 × 1m), so tick it in the catalogue if your garden is small. The colour seems to vary in intensity with soil and climate, but on average the double, quartered blooms are blush-pink with light crimson striping on the petals, fading paler after a time. Small, neat leaves, in scale with the flowers, and some thorns.

**Gloire de France** 1819. Very much one for the front of the border as it makes a low-growing, lax and spreading plant, not more than 3ft (1m) high, and about the same across. Exceptionally free with its flowers, which are very double, medium-sized and mauve-pink, fading to lilac-pink towards the petal edges. A fine rose, with the added attraction in my experience that it stays, for a Gallica, comparatively free from mildew in late summer.

**Jenny Duval** A 4ft × 3ft (1.2 × 1m) bush, opening its flowers early in the summer. The very full blooms first appear from long, coiled buds, not at all typical of the Gallicas, and are of a deep cherry-crimson shading to violet-grey in the centre. When they are fully open the bases of the petals can be seen to be a creamy-yellow, blending in with the yellow stamens. Fragrant and long-lasting.

**Officinalis** This rose we have already discussed in the introduction to this chapter, but it was not mentioned then that it is almost certainly the Red Rose of Lancaster, having been adopted by the 1st Earl of Lancaster as his badge. Certainly it is a very ancient rose indeed and forms a low but reasonably upright bush about 4ft × 4ft (1.2 × 1.2m), with only the rather slender but well-branched outer canes spreading it wider on occasion. If on its own roots it will sucker freely. The 2½in (6cm) flowers are semi-double and of a fiery crimson-pink with pale yellow stamens, fading to a rather purplish crimson, and are carried well clear of the leaves so that they give a really dazzling display. See Pl. 1.

**Perle des Panachées** 1845. Also sometimes known as 'Cottage Maid', which should not be confused with 'Village Maid', a one-time popular name for that other Gallica 'Rosa Mundi' (see below) and for several other roses as well. Light green leaves, coppery when young, on a small, moderately lax bush reaching 3ft × 3ft (1 × 1m). The blooms are about halfway between double and semi-double and are rather loosely formed, almost white, with vivid splashes and stripes of crimson. See Pl. 4.

**Président de Sèze** Madame Hébert, some time prior to 1836. This is something very special, for the double, scented, 4in (10cm) flowers open to reveal a deep, purplish-crimson centre paling dramatically into an outer circle of soft lilac-pink – a remarkable sight when the sturdy 4ft × 3ft (1.2 × 1m) bush is blooming at its peak. Larger and broader leaves than is usual with this family.

**Rosa Mundi** (R. *gallica versicolor*) A striped sport from 'Officinalis', to which the odd branch occasionally reverts, and first recorded in 1581. It is said to be named after Fair Rosamund, the mistress of Henry II, but as his dates are 1154–89, one must, with some reluctance, concede that this could be legend. At any rate, whatever its age, it is one of the most showy and gayest of the old garden roses. Blooming over a long period, it has flowers of deep pink, splashed and striped on to the palest of blush-pink backgrounds – or the other way round if you prefer. They are loosely formed, semi-double and open flat, with the petals attractively waved. The bush is compact and upright, about 4ft × 4ft (1.2 × 1.2m), but regrettably I have never yet seen it without mildew from late midsummer onwards.

**Surpasse Tout** Prior to 1832. Despite its name not perhaps the best of the Gallicas, but a good one nevertheless. The 3in (7.5cm) double flowers come very close to scarlet – a colour not known among the old garden roses – but are more precisely a brilliant cerise-pink, veined a darker shade and fading a little with age, the many petals reflexing nicely and infolded in the centre to a button eye. It is a sturdy and bushy grower to about 4–5ft (1.2–1.5m) and as much across.

**Tricolore de Flandre** Van Houtte, 1846. A small, 3ft (1m) bush with large and very double flowers of creamy-white, splashed and striped with soft purple and with a fine veining of carmine on the cream. The petals are small and multitudinous, the outer ones folding back as the flower opens, so that the blooms become pompons of great beauty.

**Tuscany Superb** A superior and slightly larger form of the very similar 'Tuscany' and first recorded in 1848. A typical upright, bushy Gallica, about 4ft × 3ft (1.2 × 1m), the double flowers opening flat and of a blackish crimson with a glimpse of golden stamens. Sometimes there may be a white streak or two on some of the petals, but unusually for a rose of such a deep red colouring there is very little scent. It will outsucker most others of the family if grown on its own roots.

*Chapter 4*

# The Damasks

Dɪᴅ these come to the West from Damascus and its environs? Were they brought back by the returning Crusaders in the thirteenth or fourteenth centuries? The answer to the first question is: probably. The answer to the second is: maybe. Nobody knows for certain, but at any rate they were in western Europe early in the sixteenth century, though by that time they were well established in Italy and other Mediterranean regions, for descriptions by Roman writers such as Pliny the Elder of the roses they knew tie in well with what we know of the Damasks today. It is, however, beyond doubt that a number of them have been used for some hundreds of years in Turkey and the mountain valleys of Bulgaria and the Balkans generally for the distillation of attar of roses. Scent is a notable characteristic of the family.

One variety it seems more than probable the Romans knew is the 'Autumn Damask' or 'Quatre Saisons' rose, the only rose of any kind known in the West that made some attempt, even if a rather fitful one, to produce more blooms in the autumn after the midsummer flush. This was to make it one of the most important varieties in rose history, for much later, in the nineteenth century, by combining accidentally with a remontant rose from China, it helped to produce the truly repeat-flowering garden roses we enjoy today. How this actually happened will be gone into in more detail in the chapter on the China roses, for this was the group created by the union.

Apart from this one and its white sport, 'Quatre Saisons Blanc Mousseux' (the last word of the name meaning it sported moss as well as white flowers), all the Damasks flower only in midsummer, mostly in various shades of pink, though 'Madame Hardy' is a notable white one and R. ×*damascena versicolor*, the York and Lancaster rose, has petals sometimes blush-pink and sometimes a

49

much stronger pink – almost red – in the same flower. It is not a striped variety like other old garden roses, though there is the same overall multicolour effect when seen from a distance.

This is a very variable family so far as growth and size are concerned, with varieties suitable for any size of garden and ranging from 'Leda' at 3ft (1m) up to 'Trigintipetala' at 7ft (2.1m) or so. Just the same, there are a number of points the Damasks do have in common. Their growth is robust but more spreading than a typical Gallica and the well-branched shoots arch naturally, especially when bearing the weight of the clusters of flowers. The flower stalks or pedicels are not themselves of the strongest, so that often the blooms nod downwards. The hips, not in most cases a notable decorative feature, are long and narrow. Downy foliage is typical of the group, as are strong, hooked thorns.

Good soil is needed to get the best from Damask roses, though they do not fare badly in most places. After flowering, twiggy growths should be thinned out and other side shoots cut back by about two thirds to encourage new ones to develop for the following year's crop of bloom. Many people find that they get quite satisfactory results without even doing this, but in my experience it does help if one wants to achieve the maximum display of flowers. Otherwise, all that is needed is the removal of dead wood as it occurs, and if the rose becomes straggly and needs bushing out, the occasional cutting back of a main cane by about one third so that you get branching lower down.

**Blush Damask** A 5ft × 6ft (1.5 × 1.8m) shrub which flowers in great profusion at midsummer, though over a shorter period than some of the others. While the blooms are there, however, they are some of the most striking of all, fully double and quartered, nodding, and reflexing into balls of deep lilac-pink, paler at the edges of the petals. A very twiggy bush with dark green leaves.

**Celsiana** Prior to 1750. Large, 4in (10cm), loosely formed semi-double flowers in great profusion, the petals of each having a transparent texture and being of a lovely rose-pink, deeper in the bud, and with a strong fragrance and yellow anthers. It makes a vigorous 5ft × 4ft (1.5 × 1.2m) bush, flowering at midsummer, and with smooth greyish leaves.

**Hebe's Lip** (R. × *damascena rubrotincta*, 'Reine Blanche', 'Margined Hip') 1912. Coming from red-tinted buds the flowers, 3in (7.5cm) across, cupped in shape, open semi-double and creamy-white with light crimson petal edges in much the same way as those of the modern climber 'Handel'. The effect is most pleasing, though it should be added that this is not a rose with a long flowering season. The darkish leaves show off the flowers well, on a reasonably sturdy, thorny, twiggy bush which will reach 4ft × 3ft (1.2 × 1m).

**Ispahan** Before 1832 (probably well before). With a much longer flowering season than others in this group, this is one of the best Damasks to grow. The large clusters of loosely semi-double blooms are a clear soft pink, about 3½in (9cm) across and are very freely borne on a sturdy, upright, bushy plant with grey-green leaves. On reflexing after a time, the flowers give the impression of having far more petals than is, in fact, the case. It was not until I examined one of them closely that I realised they were not fully double. One of the best shrub roses for any size of garden, for while it may in time reach 6ft (1.8m) in height it will keep reasonably compact. See Pl. 4.

**La Ville de Bruxelles** Vibert, 1849. The sheer weight of the clustered blooms arch out the sturdy, well-branched, 5ft (1.5m) canes so that the spread of this rose, with its fine, luxuriant foliage, is fully 4ft (1.2m). The very double flowers, quartered and with a button eye nestling amidst the short centre petals, keep their clear, soft pink and there is very little fade. Fragrant. See Pl. 4.

**Leda** Probably early in the nineteenth century, but the origin is uncertain. A compact grower to about 3ft (1m) and as much across, producing enchanting flowers from the most unpromising-looking buds. The flowers, which are double and reflex fully, retaining their rounded shape, are creamy-white and with irregular carmine flecks on the petal edges, a characteristic which has given this rose its second name of 'Painted Damask'. Dark green leaves make a perfect background for the blooms. See Pl. 5.

**Madame Hardy** Hardy, 1832. While I am prepared to put up an argument in favour of one or two others, many people think that this has the most beautiful blooms of all the old roses. They open from buds with long, feathery calyces and are sometimes blush-tinted at first. Fully expanded they are of the purest white, flat and quartered, with a green carpel in the centre. This is not a feature confined to 'Madame Hardy', but against the whiteness of the surrounding petals it is extremely distinctive. The flowers come on side shoots which are often long and may be weighed down by the size of the clusters. They are not fond of rain, but last otherwise over a long period. It grows to some 5–6ft (1.5–1.8m) and is generally reckoned to spread out about the same distance. I have seen it do this, but my personal experience of it is that it stays much more upright and compact. Matt, light to mid-green leaves which are not proof against mildew. Sweet scent. See Pl. 5.

**Quatre Saisons** Also known as the 'Autumn Damask', this was one of the roses the Romans grew. Principally of historical interest, as we have seen in the introduction to this chapter, for the double pink flowers are of poor form, though they do keep going fitfully after the midsummer flush. Not a very large bush, about 4ft × 3ft (1.2 × 1m), with light green, rather downy leaves. See Pl. 1.

**St Nicholas** The date of the discovery of this one, 1950, may or may not mislead as to its true age. All one can say is that it was discovered in that year growing in a Yorkshire garden, and whether it is a modern hybrid or a rediscovery of something very much older nobody can be certain. The 5in (13cm) semi-double, cupped flowers are very showy, deep pink with golden stamens and with red hips to follow. Reaching about 4ft (1.2m) in height and spreading out to the same distance, it may need a little attention from the secateurs after flowering to keep it shapely.

**Trigintipetala** (R. ×damascena trigintipetala) Graham Thomas identified this as one of the original Damasks, certainly of very great age, and one of the chief roses used over the centuries at Kazanlik in Bulgaria for the production of attar of roses. It is sometimes listed under the name 'Kazanlik', but as far as my own observations have gone there would appear to be two very similar roses, 'Kazanlik' being of a deeper pink and having more petals, though otherwise identical. One may be a form of the other.

I respectfully disagree with Mr Thomas, however, when he says that it is of no great garden interest. Mine came from a cutting from a roadside hedge in Greece and I did not know what it was at the time. Now it is a 7ft (2.1m) shrub, arching out all round to about 6ft (1.8m) with soft green leaves and, at the time of writing (early spring), clusters of small, narrow buds with long, feathery sepals. These will soon open to fairly large, double, loosely formed, pink and scented flowers in considerable profusion and carried over a long period. It may not have the profligacy of something like 'Nevada', which at times seems to have more blooms than it knows what to do with, but it does put on a fine show provided that any pruning is carried out straight away after flowering, giving new wood for next year's blooms plenty of time to develop. It makes a larger shrub than any of the other Damasks, but it is reasonably open and not too dense in habit. See Pl. 5.

**York and Lancaster** (R. ×*damascena versicolor*) Put it at the sixteenth century or earlier. Often confused, even by those who should know better, with R. *gallica versicolor*, which is 'Rosa Mundi', a very different rose. Though both have pink and blush-white flowers, 'York and Lancaster' is nothing like so free-blooming and its loosely double flowers are not often striped. They are, rather, parti-coloured, some blooms being pink, some almost pure white, and some with both pink and white petals. In a hot summer it performs reasonably well and on good soils will form a big, vigorous shrub of 6ft × 6ft (1.8 × 1.8m). It is of special interest in that it may be the rose referred to in Shakespeare's *Henry IV, Part 2*, when the rival factions were choosing their emblems for the Wars of the Roses in the Temple Gardens. Almost certainly grown by the then Vicar of Bray.

*Chapter 5*

# The Albas

ONE of the oldest and also one of the loveliest of the old rose families. There are not all that many of them, but they do make up in the quality both of their flowers and their foliage what they may lack in quantity. Of uncertain origin, they go back at least to Greek and Roman times and may well have been brought to western Europe, including the United Kingdom, by the conquering Roman armies. They became naturalised, in the north of England particularly, and one of them became well enough known to be chosen as the White Rose of York and another as Bonnie Prince Charlie's Jacobite Rose.

From their name one would imagine that all the Albas were white, but in fact this seems only to apply to the very early ones, the later hybrids being various shades of pink. Botanical indications point to a Damask × R. *corymbifera* parentage, so despite their Latin name they are all hybrids. The first cross must have occurred centuries ago, for the Danish hybridist, the late Svend Poulsen, reported some Albas (though he did not specify which, unfortunately) coming true from seed, in effect having become new species roses.

Albas are included among several types of rose – coming second only to the Damasks – used for the production of attar of roses and, together with the Centifolias, can be found in the flower paintings of the seventeenth-century Dutch masters. They have made a considerable impact in a number of fields over the years.

As garden shrubs the Albas take some beating. Some are large, some are comparatively small, and all have clusters of scented flowers with petals short and tough enough to be reasonably resistant to rain (which cannot be said of all the old rose families). All have strong, vigorous growth, and all have fine grey-green leaves which make them an asset even when the blooms have

54

vanished with the passing of summer. The substantial canes keep upright so support is not often needed, and though they have fairly substantial hooked thorns, these are generally few in number so that cutting out old dead wood or shortening laterals after flowering, which is all the attention the Albas need, is not usually a painful process. One or two of them bear very worthwhile hips and, while many an old member of the rose family has adopted the philosophy of Marcus Aurelius when it comes to mildew – 'It is part of the destiny of the Universe ordained for you from the beginning. All that befalls you is part of the great web' – the Albas will have none, or at any rate very little, of this kind of thinking.

The Albas are upright growers, but the larger ones will still cover a lot of ground because of their sheer size. However, as there are also some smaller varieties, a suitable Alba can be chosen for almost any spot in the garden: for specimens (though once-flowering); for a mixed shrub rose planting; for planting mixed in with other shrubs (provided they are allowed their share of sun) where their fine leaves will add distinction, and for hedges. They will spread freely by suckers if on their own roots or if they are planted more deeply than usual, though at an easily controllable rate. An occasional chop down with a spade will keep things under control.

**R. × alba maxima** This, the Jacobite Rose, is one of the really old ones and is also known as the Great Double White. It forms a huge 7ft × 8ft (2.1 × 2.4m) shrub, with the typical grey-green leaves of the family. In total, one of the most handsome roses there is, with a fine, upright carriage and strong growth. At midsummer, the flat, double, creamy-white flowers appear, sometimes with blush tints in the folds of the petals at first. They are fragrant and followed by oval hips. It can be effectively used as a wall shrub and does not mind a north wall, but it is just as good in a mixed shrub planting or standing as a specimen on its own. Though the flowers come only once, there is a long succession of them over many weeks.

**R. × alba semi-plena** Also very ancient and dating certainly from before 1600, this is thought to be the White Rose of York. In general similar to R. × alba maxima (though it may grow even bigger), except that the clusters of flowers are smaller and only

55

semi-double, again white and with golden stamens. Showy hips
follow them. See Pl. 5.

**Belle Amour** Salmon-pink, semi-double, cupped blooms with
orange-yellow stamens, growing in clusters on a strong, upright
bush of about 6ft × 4ft (1.8 × 1.2m) with good hips to follow.
Slight, spicy scent and typical Alba leaves.

**Celestial** Also known as 'Céleste', this one will go up to 6ft
(1.8m) and spread out to about 7ft (2.1m), which means it is a more
lax grower than most of the family. The half-open buds are of exceptional beauty and open to almost transparent, soft pink, shell-
like, semi-double flowers which look wonderful against the blue-
grey leaves. They come in clusters of two or three and have a rich
scent. One of the best of all, resulting in an AM in 1948. See Pl. 6.

**Félicité Parmentier** In cultivation since 1834. One for the smaller
garden and not usually exceeding 4ft (1.2m) by about 3ft (1m),
though I have seen it bigger. I have tried in vain to find out why so
many roses show red in the bud and then open out to flowers of
every other colour under the sun. Well, here is one that breaks
with tradition, for the buds are the palest primrose yellow, before
turning into very double pompon-style flowers of the palest pink,
though it must be admitted that there can be a hint of creamy-
yellow in them at times. The plant is quite bushy, but, like
'Celestial', is also fairly spreading. See Pl. 6.

**Great Maiden's Blush** Very old and from prior to the fifteenth
century at least. Among a whole string of names gathered over
the years, including R. × *alba incarnata*, it was known in France at
one time as *Cuisse de Nymphe Émue*, or Thigh of the Passionate
Nymph. The only possible reason I can think of for not reverting
to this wonderful name is that it could lead to misunderstandings
when ordering, but it is no bad choice to describe the clusters of
very double, mother-of-pearl blooms, though they tend to fade
almost to white. This rose will grow to 6ft (1.8m) in time –
sometimes more if it is happy in its site – by about 5ft (1.5m) and is
the last of the Albas to come into bloom, continuing after the
others are over. Sweet scent. See also 'Maiden's Blush' below.

**Königin von Danemarck** On occasion to be found in nursery lists under the translation of its name, 'Queen of Denmark', this rose may be a Damask–Alba hybrid and dates from 1826. It is probably the best Alba for medium-sized gardens, growing on average to 5ft × 4ft (1.5 × 1.2m). Small gardeners (or owners of small gardens) can rejoice, however, for it is also one of the loveliest of the family, the carmine-pink buds opening and gradually reflexing to very double, sometimes quartered blooms of a soft rose pink, with a button eye and a sweet scent. They keep coming for weeks and weeks and stand up to rain remarkably well for flowers with a great many petals. Fairly open and lax in habit, it has the typically blue-grey leaves of the group. See Pl. 6.

**Madame Legras de St Germain** The dates given for the first introduction of this rose vary between a definite 1846 and prior to 1840. Hardly enough variation to give anyone sleepless nights, but one more indication of how uncertain we are about such things. A date may seem to be firmly established for a rose, and then an even earlier mention of it suddenly comes to light. This is one of the larger Albas, growing sturdily and with long, almost thornless shoots reaching up to 6ft (1.8m) or so and arching out to about the same, with the usual grey-green leaves. The many short petals mean that the flowers open cupped, creamy-white with, until it fades in the sun, a yellow flush in the centre. Camellia-like in effect, the tissue paper petals are not at all happy in the rain, though a fine fragrance goes some way to make up for this when the sun shines.

**Madame Plantier** Plantier 1835. Probably an Alba × Musk rose, there is some doubt as to which group this rose should belong to, but if well tended and on good soil it will go shinning up a low tree or tall bush to 12ft (3.7m) or so, or it will make a dense, arching bush of 6ft × 6ft (1.8 × 1.8m). The small, light green leaves give away the rose's mongrel ancestry, though in fact they are not typical of either of the supposed parent families. Botanists must have found other pointers. The blooms at midsummer come in large clusters, each a smallish pompon, creamy-white and fading to pure white, with a green carpel in the centre. Suitably trained, it will make a good 4–5ft (1.2–1.5m) hedge.

**Maiden's Blush**  The smaller of the two 'Maiden's Blush' roses referred to above, generally similar to its bigger sister but only reaching a height of 5ft (1.5m) or so. The 2½in (6cm) flowers open quite flat and, though I have not actually sat down and counted them, there would seem to be fewer petals than there are in the other rose. Both are featured in early flower paintings.

*Chapter 6*

# The Centifolias

JUST where the Centifolias came from in the first place is a matter of some doubt, though it may have been eastern Europe or the Near East. There is confusion, too, in the name itself, in that centifolia actually means one hundred leaves and it is petals that are being referred to. However, the latter point has a ready if not particularly satisfactory explanation. One has only to look through an old plant book such as Gerarde's *Herball* of the seventeenth century to realise that in those days petals were, as often as not, referred to as leaves. Gerarde also, rather intriguingly, called the stamens of a flower chives.

Roman writers such as Pliny the Elder in his *Natural History* and some others mention Centifolia roses, though from the descriptions they give it does seem unlikely that they were of the same family as the one we know under that name. They obviously had roses with many petals, but then that is not such a rarity among the old varieties and the word Centifolia could have been used in a loose kind of way to describe most of them, without getting down to actual counting, just as we use the word 'double'. At any rate, the group we know today as the Centifolias, though without doubt of considerable age, can only be traced back with anything remotely approaching certainty to a period considerably after the Roman heyday.

It was rose growers in the Netherlands who first recognised their merits some time in the seventeenth century and who were largely responsible for their development. This must have meant in the main increasing the number of varieties through the careful selection of sports, because with so many petals permanently enveloping their reproductive organs it was (and is) rare for a Centifolia to set seed.

From Holland they spread across the Channel to the United

Kingdom, and were also welcomed with such enthusiasm in France that their earlier popular name of Holland roses fell into disuse, to be replaced by that of Provence roses or Rose of Provence. This is still used and leads to no end of confusion with, as we have seen, the Gallica or Provins Rose. Centifolias are also the original cabbage roses, though only perhaps resembling cabbages when they are about three quarters open.

Apart from a few of the smaller ones such as 'De Meaux' and 'Petite de Hollande', it cannot be said that the Centifolias are ideal shrubs for the lazy gardener. They need help to give of their best, for they tend to be rangy, rather lax and far from bushy growers, and the weight of the sumptuous, scented blooms will bear the canes right down to the ground unless they are given some kind of support by careful staking or by using pillars or tripods for the tallest varieties. Since in many cases a weakness in the neck also causes the flowers to nod, getting them up as high as possible, even if artificially, enables one to appreciate their beauty fully without actually having to lie on your back. The outer petals of a typical Centifolia are large and enfold the closely packed and much shorter central ones. Thus protected, these retain their full depth of colouring, at any rate until, with some of them, the whole bloom reflexes into a ball.

The leaves of the family are large and drooping, and sadly mildew will spread from one to another like gossip unless steps are taken to prevent it. New shoots four or five feet long may develop during one season: these may be shortened by about a third to half in early spring to encourage side branches or laterals to grow and give the bushes some semblance of shape. Side shoots can be reduced by about one third at the same time.

**The Bishop** Of unknown age and origin. One of the few Centifolias that will stay naturally upright, reaching 5ft × 3ft (1.5 × 1m), for though fairly slender-looking it does not need anything to lean on. The flowers are by no means typical of the family, coming in clusters of rosette-shaped blooms in cerise-purple with a lilac reverse, fading overall to lilac-mauve with distinct bluish tones. Early-flowering and with un-Centifolia-like glossy leaves.

**Bullata** Two dates are given, 1801 and prior to 1815. With its large, double, globular pink blooms, this is in all respects except one almost identical to the original 'Centifolia' itself, which is described next. It differs only in having much larger, drooping leaves, so wrinkled that they resemble those of a lettuce.

**Centifolia** The original Cabbage Rose, Rose of a Hundred Leaves, and also called Rose des Peintres, having been a favourite model for the Dutch artists of the seventeenth century. My general description of the family characteristics fits this one exactly, and the huge, globular, scented blooms are of a soft pink. It will reach 5ft (1.5m) and spread out as far as you will let it within those limits when the canes lean over.

**Chapeau de Napoléon** (*R. × centifolia cristata*)  Introduced by Vibert in 1827 as 'Crested Moss', which was not really surprising except that it is not a true Moss rose. Mossing only occurs on the edges and tips of the calyces, but it does give the buds a unique, crested look. When they are partly open there is some resemblance to the French Emperor's hat, which is the reason for this rose's other common name. An oddity, whichever way you look at it, but the rich rose-pink flowers themselves are more conventional. Globular at first, they open quite flat with many of them quartered, on a bush about 5ft × 4ft (1.5 × 1.2m) which is perhaps rather more slender and graceful than the type. See Pl. 6.

**De Meaux** Sweet, 1789. Once again we depart from the norm, because this forms a reasonably erect though still arching bush which is only about 3ft 6in (107cm) in height and with small, light green leaves. The soft pink flowers are small, only about 1in (2.5cm) across, and pass from globular to the pompon stage before finishing up flat. Sweetly scented, they come fairly early and will be even more freely produced if the bush is reasonably hard pruned and the twiggy growth thinned out every year. Plenty of canes come from the base and they branch well. See Pl. 7.

**Fantin-Latour** To adapt a saying of Martin Luther, 'Even if I knew the world was going to end tomorrow, I would plant "Fantin-Latour" just the same.' From which you can gather that, if my taste is as good as I like to think it is, this is one of the most beautiful roses of all. The 3½in (9cm) flowers open roughly cup-shaped, but soon the petals reflex to show a button eye. Of the

61

softest pink, they come in clusters small and large with tremendous profusion and over many weeks. The bush is very sturdy with strong canes, and with the minimum of help from a stake will keep quite compact and reach up to 7ft (2.1m). If there is no restraint it will certainly spread out, but it will keep itself under control and its flowers out of the mud. Dark, smooth, handsome leaves which, much as I would like to deny it, are not resistant to mildew. AM 1959, AGM 1968. See Pl. 7.

**Juno**  Prior to 1832. Fittingly named after the Queen of the Gods of Roman legend, even though, in the person of Hera in her earlier Greek incarnation, Paris judged her to be second best in beauty to Aphrodite. The fragrant, petal-filled, blush-pink blooms, globular in the bud and opening flat with a button eye, can only be fully appreciated if the canes on which they grow are supported. Perhaps it was posture that influenced Paris, for Juno is a lax and rather rangy grower, but will look fine on a pillar or tripod, the shoots reaching 5–6ft (1.5–1.8m) in length. Striking dull green leaves.

**Petite de Hollande**  1817. Without doubt the best of the smaller members of this group, self-supporting and fairly bushy. The canes do arch outwards, but the clusters of sweetly scented 2½in (6cm) flowers are not of sufficient weight to change this to the Centifolia sprawl. Pale pink, which deepens towards the centre, they are exact counterparts in miniature of their bigger relatives. The rather coarsely toothed – or 'snipt', as Gerarde puts it – leaves are scaled down in the same way and are perfectly in keeping. At 4ft (1.2m) rather larger than 'De Meaux', but both will do for foreground planting in a shrubbery.

**Robert le Diable**  An untidy grower due to its rather weak branches. They will reach 4ft (1.2m), but badly need their elbows on something to keep the flowers from exchanging confidences with the weeds. The blooms would indicate by their form that a Gallica figures somewhere in the background, as they are not globular and the petals quickly reflex. They are extremely striking, a rich purple with slate-blue and violet shadings, with the odd centre petal sometimes a vivid cerise or scarlet in startling contrast.

**Spong** 1805. One of the smaller Centifolias and more bushy and compact than most, to be classed for size with 'Petite de Hollande' at about 4ft × 3ft (1.2 × 1m). It is probably the first of the group into flower in early summer, the small, double blooms being a rich pink. Scented, they tend to lose their charm as they age, making dead-heading something of a must. If I thought for a very long time I could hardly come up with a less attractive name than 'Spong', but as it is said to be that of the man who raised this rose, or at least discovered it, one can only shrug and accept it.

**Tour de Malakoff** Soupert and Notting, 1856. This is one of the really big ones, with heavy, arching branches reaching 6ft (1.8m) in length so that they need a tough prop – preferably a pillar. It also needs good soil to do well, but once again some extra effort is more than worthwhile for the sake of the flowers. These are huge – 5in (13cm) or so across – loosely double and of a vivid carmine with lilac edging to the petals when newly opened, the carmine changing gradually through violet to a bluish, dusky grey before the petals fall. It is a breathtaking transformation.

*Chapter 7*

# The Moss Roses

THERE are, in fact, two groups of Moss roses, those which have sported from the Centifolias, and the far less numerous Damask Mosses. Both originated as sports, and the reversion of an odd branch or two to its Centifolia or Damask form occurs now and then, more often with some varieties than others. If a rose shows occasional signs of going backwards like this, it can be useful in tracing the intricacies of its history. This is especially the case if it is the flower that reverts and not just the moss, as occurred with the Damask Moss 'Quatre Saisons Blanc Mousseux', which turned out to be a white, mossy sport of the pink 'Quatre Saisons', the 'Autumn Damask'. A sport, for those who do not know, is a mutation, in which in most cases one of the characteristics of an ancestor of a certain variety suddenly appears again and causes a radical change, either to some of the flowers on a bush or in the case of climbing sports to the habit of growth. Sports can be propagated from by budding, but are not always completely stable and may, as we have seen, revert. Moss roses are a little different from most sports in that the moss probably first appeared as a straight mutation having no reference to the past.

Being so closely related to the Centifolias, most of the general points I have made about the character and treatment of these apply equally to the first of the two groups of Moss roses. Some of them are perhaps a little more bushy, and a few do produce a scattering of late bloom after the midsummer flush, but the distinctive thing about them is, of course, the moss. This consists of green, reddish and sometimes brown glandular projections all over the flower stalks and sepals. These are sticky and fragrant, and a bare description of this sort does not make them sound particularly attractive.My own feeling is that they are not and I cannot see that they add anything to the beauty of a rose. Never-

64

theless, the old-world associations with Victorian cottage gardens and valentines cannot be ignored and explain the affection for these roses that many people have. I like them despite the moss.

Like the Centifolias, Moss roses came from Holland about two hundred years ago. The colour range covers white, all shades of pink, crimson and maroon-purple – all the old garden rose colours, in fact – and there is a modern yellow one called 'Golden Moss'. The American breeder Ralph Moore has recently succeeded in breeding miniature Moss roses, a considerable achievement because Moss roses are just as reluctant as the Centifolias to set seed.

The Centifolia Mosses like good cultivation and should have some of the old shoots cut back fairly hard each year after flowering, as the best blooms come in growth of the previous summer. Provided that you are prepared to attempt your own budding, for you will not get them from a nursery except as a special (and expensive) order, Moss roses (and for that matter a number of the other old garden roses) make most effective standards. Ask anyone whose memory goes back to Victorian times, when standards were much more popular than they are today. Cuttings can be taken in autumn and root easily.

For small to average-sized gardens almost any of the Moss roses are suitable, even the huge 'William Lobb' or 'Jeanne de Montfort', if these are used as pillar roses or short climbers. On all of them keep an eye open for the first signs of mildew and deal with it promptly.

The Damask Mosses, though some of them can reach a considerable size, are on the whole more compact and freely branching. The white sport of the 'Autumn Damask' mentioned above appears in the parentage of many of them and has passed on its much coarser moss which is more prickly to the touch and generally turns brown, even if it starts out green.

**Blanche Moreau** Moreau-Robert, 1880. The parents were 'Comtesse de Murinais' × 'Quatre Saisons Blanc Mousseux' so that we start off with a Damask Moss. The family influence of both parents shows only to any marked degree in the rather spiky, brownish moss. The lax and very prickly stems will go up to 5ft (1.5m) if supported on a pillar, and without this help a rather sprawling bush will result. Exceptionally dark green leaves and stems, with brown thorns, contrast vividly with the double, 3in (7.5cm), creamy-white flowers, which are carried in clusters but which are only slightly fragrant. The occasional flower in late summer probably comes from 'Autumn Damask' heritage.

**Capitaine John Ingram** Laffay, 1854. This is a rather late-flowering and bushy shrub which will reach 5ft × 4ft (1.5 × 1.2m). It has dark green leaves and small, full-petalled, rosette-shaped flowers of wine-purple with a lighter reverse. Apart from the button eye, they look like small peonies, fragrant and with dark red moss on the buds and flower stalks.

**Common Moss** ('Old Pink Moss') One of the earliest, probably first appeared in France about 1696. It is sometimes said to be the original Centifolia Moss sport, R. × *centifolia muscosa*, but I think that it is much more likely to be the first to be widely distributed, since the first Mosses did not come from France. Anyway, whether they are the same or not, there is no later variety which can excel it in the beauty of its very double, globular and later flat, pink blooms with their sweet scent. A 5ft × 4ft (1.5 × 1.2m) bush of typical Centifolia habit can be expected. Long calyces on the buds and reddish moss.

**Comtesse de Murinais** Vibert, 1843. Certainly one for a pillar or tripod, as it will go up to 6ft (1.8m) and, if unsupported, make a far from graceful plant. Probably a Damask rose has given it this extra vigour, another clue to parentage coming in the rather rough moss, even if this is green instead of the brownish-green one would expect. With strict discipline from the gardener this is a rose that will put on a fine show, the many double flowers opening flat and full of petals and often quartered. The blush-pink fades gradually almost to white. Fine scent.

**Duchesse de Verneuil** Portemer, 1856. Smallish flowers, but making up for their lack of size with their showiness, for they are of a strong pink, lighter on the reverse and with a button eye. A 5ft (1.5m) bush, spreading out well.

**Général Kléber** Robert, 1856. In habit similar to the Duchesse above, but the flowers are up to 5in (13cm) across. They are of mother-of-pearl pink and have a silky sheen to them, opening flat

and showing a button eye. The moss and the leaves are bright
green. Rich fragrance.

**Gloire des Mousseux** Laffay, 1852. The 1850s seem to have been
vintage years for the Moss roses and also produced this one, a
robust plant about 4ft × 4ft (1.2 × 1.2m) with plentiful light green
leaves and light green moss, which sometimes spreads quite a long
way down the stems. Richly scented, the flowers are probably the
biggest of all the Mosses, a clear pink with infolded centres and
button eyes. The colour fades slowly to a pale blush-pink. See
Pl. 7.

**Henri Martin** Laffay, 1863. Coming into flower a little later than
most, the clusters of medium-sized double blooms are of a vivid
light crimson, a much stronger colour than any of the others we
have dealt with so far and one that will make a contrasting splash
in a mixed planting. It makes a very thorny bush about 5ft × 4ft
(1.5 × 1.2m) with fine, bright green leaves, but the moss on the
buds tends to be sparse. See Pl. 7.

**James Mitchell** Verdier, 1861. A strong-growing but not over-
large bush, achieving on average 5ft × 5ft (1.5 × 1.5m), the flowers
coming freely along the arching canes. Though not too large they
come with tremendous profusion, neatly rounded, double, and
opening to purplish-pink pompons which fade to lilac-pink. Early
into flower and with brownish moss.

**Jeanne de Montfort** Robert, 1851. Another from the 1850s and,
as we already know, to be classed with 'William Lobb' for its tall,
rangy growth, which may produce 8ft (2.4m) canes that can only
be coped with on a pillar or wall. The scented, pink, semi-double
flowers, appearing in clusters, are loosely informal, so that one can
catch a glimpse of yellow stamens, a rare sight in the Centifolia
group. The flowers will fade to a lighter colour after a while, but
there may sometimes be a few in the autumn as a bonus. They are
strongly scented and the buds are exceptionally heavily mossed.

**Madame Delaroche-Lambert** Robert, 1851. Rich, purple-
crimson, double flowers with an even more intense colouring in
the centre and with little tendency to fade, even in strong sun. It

67

makes a more bushy plant than many mosses, and the moss itself on the flower stems and long sepals is particularly abundant. Occasional blooms may come late in the year. 4ft × 3ft (1.2 × 1m).

**Mousseline** ('Alfred de Dalmas') Portemer, 1855. Unwonted energy for a Moss rose, in that the flowers, after the first grand flush in early summer, appear with reasonable continuity right through until autumn. They are medium-sized to large, double and cup-shaped, of a soft flesh-pink and sweetly fragrant. The buds have short, brownish-green moss and the bush rarely tops 4ft (1.2m) with a spread of about the same.

**Nuits de Young** Laffay, 1845. By far the darkest of all the Moss roses, having neat, dark green leaves with coppery overtones and blooms which form symmetrical rosettes, singly and in clusters, of a deep, velvety maroon, which fades little as the blooms age. Yellow stamens may be glimpsed and the moss is dark and brownish-red, sometimes touched with purple. Strong fragrance. An erect, wiry bush, slender for a Moss, about 4ft × 3ft (1.2 × 1m). Try it set against silver-leaved plants.

**Péllison** Vibert, 1848. Sometimes listed as 'Monsieur Péllison'. Small leaves for a cousin of the Centifolias, but a well-branched and fairly bushy habit make it more or less self-supporting at 4ft × 4ft (1.2 × 1.2m). The double flowers are of a strong, uniform pink, fading, but pleasingly, in time. See Pl. 7.

**William Lobb** ('Duchesse d'Istrie') Laffay, 1855. The best way to cope with this exuberant grower is to use it as a short climber, when its long canes will reach 6ft (1.8m) or more. Left to itself it will lounge inelegantly, spreading out far and wide to display its incredibly thorny stems, with clusters of bloom mainly at the ends. Properly trained there will be more flower-bearing side shoots and order will be restored. The blooms themselves are of singular beauty, very double, about 3in (7.5cm) across, and of a dark fuscia-purple and with a light magenta reverse to the petals. In time they pale to a soft lilac-grey. Very heavy mossing. See Pl. 7.

*Chapter 8*

# The Chinas

NOBODY really knows the history of cultivated roses in ancient China because under the rule of the Mandarins it was an even more closed society than it was under Chairman Mao. But though the peony and the chrysanthemum were the favourite flowers, it is certain that roses were also cultivated, for many of them were eventually brought to the West either as seeds or plants by members of political and religious missions and a few other adventurous plant collectors. These were very far removed from wild rose forms and in fact a number of them were actually bought from a famous plant nursery in Canton.

China roses had a number of qualities that had not been seen before. Crimson colouring such as is found in 'Slater's Crimson China' was one of them, and was soon introduced into the blood-stream of Western varieties. In addition, the lighter pinks had the engaging habit of blushing to a deeper colouring in hot sunshine, instead of fading to white. But above all, the roses came into bloom early and then, wonder of wonders, kept going right through to the autumn.

Just why this should be so it is impossible to say, except that a different environment can bring about, over many centuries, major changes in the habits of plants of one family, as I mentioned when discussing chance hybrids of species roses. It is even possible that Western roses were once remontant and lost the habit, rather than that the Far Eastern roses gained it. Long, cold winters over perhaps thousands of years, such as might follow an ice age, would leave no time for a second flush. Dormancy would come early and the pattern would gradually become established. However, nobody knows or is likely to know, so enough of speculation.

It was in the eighteenth century that China roses first reached the West, and though they gained some popularity as novelties, many years were to elapse before their full potential as breeding plants for a new race was realised. Compared to the Albas, Damasks, Centifolias and others they were poor, spindly growers, and not all of them were hardy. And of course in those days it was not realised that man could deliberately produce a new hybrid. It was pure chance and simply because bushes of the two roses were planted near to each other that brought about the first cross of a China rose with the 'Autumn Damask' on the Île de Bourbon in the Indian Ocean. The resulting seedlings were seen by a French botanist called Bréon, who recognised their unique qualities. The new roses became the first of the tough, vigorous and repeat-flowering Bourbons, but this did not happen until early in the nineteenth century, which makes it a very long time after the first Chinas made the long sea voyage to their new home.

Luckily for us a number of the very early China roses have survived. 'Old Blush', otherwise known as 'Parson's Pink China' and thought to be the Île de Bourbon China rose, is one. So is 'Slater's Crimson China', though it is only in comparatively recent years that it was rediscovered growing in Bermuda after having been considered lost for ever.

For a garden of limited size, most of the Chinas are ideal. Many are even suitable for bedding, but not if you want a show like a jazz festival. They have a delicacy that makes them much more suitable for planting in clumps of three or four to make a quiet focal point, for mixing in with other plants, which they do very well, or for use as patio roses in tubs. A few of them will make quite sizeable shrubs, but they still retain their light, airy habit.

Extremely healthy, narrow, pointed leaves, often of a dark, bronzy green, are a characteristic of the Chinas. Their one failing is that the extremely numerous clusters of flowers they all bear, in various shades of pink, red and crimson, are not usually noted for their scent.

They seem to do well in most soils, provided that they have a warm, sunny position. Prune to about three buds the first spring after planting, and then all that is needed in subsequent years is a little trimming back of twiggy wood in early spring and the complete removal of any that is clearly spent.

Those who are expecting to find 'Cécile Brunner', 'Perle d'Or' and others which much resemble the Chinas described below must look in the chapter on Polyanthas, where they fit more happily. A good deal of confusion is caused because nursery catalogues generally put them with the Chinas purely for convenience. There are not usually enough Polyantha or China varieties in the average catalogue nowadays to form sections on their own, and it must be said in mitigation (a little reluctantly) that purely from the point of view of garden usage the nurseries do have an argument on their side. Many Polyanthas and a number of Chinas can be used in exactly the same way.

**R. chinensis 'Major'** Despite an undertaking I made earlier, this is a rose which it may be extremely difficult to buy from a nursery. By describing it I am hoping to create a demand which may change this, for it is used as an understock for greenhouse roses and material for propagating it should not be hard to come by. My own specimens were raised from cuttings and came from Greece. Not, it must be said, completely hardy in a really cold winter (cuttings, which grow with great rapidity and vigour, if taken regularly each year will save you here if you lose an established plant), it is a very lovely, though only once-flowering rose. With its long, pliable and freely branching canes it almost has the habit of a rambler and will go up to 7ft (2.1m). It could certainly be trained on a pillar. The sheer number of shoots that come up from the base, however, make it equally suitable as a large, 6ft × 5ft (1.8 × 1.5m) shrub, with a good covering of mid-green, pointed leaves, not fully proof against mildew. The flowers, which come in great profusion and in medium-sized clusters, are large for a China rose, about 2½in (6cm) across, and of a delicate light pink, shading to blush. They are double and open cupped, keeping going for many weeks. See Pl. 8.

**Comtesse du Cayla** Guillot, 1902. Free-flowering and continuous, this is another of the larger China roses. It may well reach 5ft (1.5m) in height and, being well branched and anything but formal in its growth, spread out to 5ft (1.5m) as well. The clustered blooms are scented, semi-double, coppery-flame in the bud, and open salmon-pink with a hint of yellow on the petal reverse. All these colours will be on the bush at the same time, and would make Harlequin look dowdy. Good, dark, bronze-green leaves. Do not prune hard for the best results.

**Cramoisi Supérieur** ('Agrippina') Coquereau, 1832. Plentiful clusters of semi-double, cupped, bright crimson flowers, tending to hang their heads, on a small, twiggy bush about 3ft × 2ft (1m × 60cm). Remontant, but only very slightly scented. There is a climbing form dating from 1885 which will reach perhaps 10ft (3m).

**Fellemberg** ('La Belle Marseillaise') Fellemberg, 1857. The small, cupped blooms in large clusters are almost continuously present throughout the summer and autumn on this large, 7ft × 6ft (2.1 × 1.8m), spreading but typically open and informal shrub. The crimson buds open to the deepest pink. Good, healthy foliage. Sometimes listed as a short climber, in which form it will reach 8ft (2.4m) or so.

**Hermosa** ('Armosa', 'Mélanie Lemaire') Marcheseau, 1840. A short, well-branched, thorny, upright bush, bearing clusters of globular pink flowers. A good one for the smallest garden and useful for a low hedge. 3ft × 2ft (1m × 60cm). See Pl. 8.

**Madame Laurette Messimy** Guillot Fils, 1887. 'Rival de Paestum' × 'Madame Falcot'. From the same raiser as 'Comtesse du Cayla' and of similar stature and habit of growth. Few thorns on the freely branched canes, which bear healthy, narrow, pointed, glaucous, grey-green leaves. Constantly in flower, the clustered blooms being semi-double and coppery rose-pink, shading to yellow at the centre. See Pl. 8.

**Mutabilis** ('Tipo Ideale') Of unknown age, but almost certainly going back a century or two. Not perhaps 100 per cent hardy and undoubtedly of much greater vigour if given the protection of a warm wall. On this it can be used as a climber, usually reaching 8ft (2.4m) or so, though exceptional specimens have far exceeded this. Otherwise, it forms a 3ft (1m) well-branched, spreading bush, with fine dark, bronze-green leaves. These form a fitting background for the truly remarkable flowers which are carried from early summer until the last months of the year. Single and about 3in (7.5cm) across, they come in clusters and open from flame-coloured buds, changing to coppery-yellow which in turn fades to pink and then copper-crimson, all the colours to be seen on the bush at the
72

same time. The idea may occur that it must be similar to the Floribunda 'Masquerade' and certainly the constantly changing colours, which are roughly similar, give some substance to such a thought. However, there is no real resemblance and at no stage does 'Mutabilis' turn to the hideous dirty crimson which is the final stage of 'Masquerade'. This 'bush of butterflies' is always attractive. Gay but not garish. AM 1957. See Pl. 8.

**Old Blush** ('Parson's Pink China', 'Common Monthly Rose') This is very likely to have been the rose which, crossed with the 'Autumn Damask', produced the first Bourbon, and it is one of the most continuously in flower, often until Christmas. An upright, dainty, twiggy shrub, with clusters of flowers, shapely in the bud and opening cupped. They are double, about 2½in (6cm) across, and of a delicate pink that deepens quite markedly as the blooms age. Usually about 3ft × 4ft (1 × 1.2m). Fewer thorns than the rather similar 'Hermosa'. Reputed to be the 'Last Rose of Summer' in the old Irish song. See Pl. 1.

**Pompon de Paris** 1839. More often grown nowadays as a short climber up to about 8ft (2.4m) or so, but the bush form was a fashionable pot plant in France in the nineteenth century and is thought to be one of the ancestors of our modern miniature roses. Small, dark leaves and very twiggy growth and 1in (2.5cm) bright pink flowers in large clusters which do not, despite the rose's name, have enough petals to form true pompons. Summer flowering only, though there may be a scattering of late blooms.

**Serratipetala** ('Rose Oeillet de Saint Arguey') Vilfroy, 1912. It is not realised by most people that the Grootendorst Rugosas ('Pink Grootendorst', 'F.J. Grootendorst', etc.) are not the only roses to have their petals fringed like a pink or Sweet William. They are certainly the best known and the easiest to get hold of, but for a change (assuming you have something to change from), why not try pursuing this one through the catalogues. It makes a smaller bush than the Grootendorsts, growing only to about 5ft × 5ft (1.5 × 1.5m), and is open in habit with rather sparse leaves. The flowers are crimson, lighter in the centre, intensifying in hot weather but becoming paler in the autumn.

73

**Slater's Crimson China** (R. *chinensis semperflorens*) The China
rose that became lost and was found again, but it does originally
go back in the West to 1792. As we know, the crimson flowers
gave us our modern crimson roses, and in most ways it resembles
'Serratipetala' without the fringed petal edges. Both roses do
better if given some shelter and neither should be pruned too hard.
Old and twiggy wood may be removed in spring and shoots
formed the previous summer shortened by not more than a third.
Good scent.

***R. viridiflora*** (The Green Rose and, less kindly, R. *monstrosa*)
It is certainly an oddity, but at the same time it is not a rose that
makes its presence felt in the garden. Only a keen flower arranger
would spot it at once. It makes an open-growing bush of about
4ft × 3ft (1.2 × 1m) and is in flower in my garden longer than any
other rose, from very early spring until the turn of the year. The
leaves and bluish buds, with long, decorative calyces, give promise
of perfectly normal flowers to follow, but anyone expecting that is
in for a surprise. The blooms open with somewhat confused leafy
green 'petals' which quite soon become streaked haphazardly with
brown and purple. They are not petals at all in the usual sense of
the word and the rose is obviously a mutation from some China
rose of the past. Nobody knows its origin, but it has been in
cultivation for certain since 1833.

## Chapter 9

# The Bourbons and Portlands

RUDYARD Kipling was wrong. As we have seen when discussing China roses, East did meet West in a most satisfactory way when a China rose and the 'Autumn Damask' came together to produce the first Bourbon. Strong-growing, tough, with large, full-petalled flowers and in the majority of cases producing a second crop of bloom in the autumn, it was no wonder that the new race rapidly supplanted practically everything else and reigned supreme in Western gardens for over fifty years until the coming of the Hybrid Perpetuals. Their colours blend well with the older Gallicas, Albas and Damasks and cover much the same range. The flowers of most varieties are crammed with petals and are often scented. There is a main flush of bloom at midsummer, but you must pick your roses wisely if you want anything worthwhile later on. Some varieties are as good or even better in autumn, but there are a few that simply do not repeat at all. Blooms come on the current year's wood as well as on the old, in which the Bourbons differ from the majority of the roses from earlier periods.

There is a considerable difference in the way the various Bourbons grow, but most will send strong canes up to 5–6ft (1.5–1.8m) and spread out to 4ft (1.2m) or so, branching freely, so that they must be allowed plenty of space. Training on a pillar or tripod of rustic poles is the best way to curb their natural exuberance. But as they have far from pliable canes, it is as well for this to be started from the very beginning if it is not to become a thorny wrestling match between the grower and the rose. This does not always apply, however, and three of the very best, 'La Reine Victoria', 'Madame Pierre Oger' and 'Louise Odier' are much more amenable. Their canes may reach the same length as the others, but they are slender and lax. Support for them is essential, not to control them, but so that their lovely, globular blooms can be displayed properly and not hang down, their faces hidden.

Pruning of the Bourbons is not essential if you have room to let them spread. Many people just leave them alone, but if you do decide to carry it out, and I think that you get more and better flowers if you do, spur back side shoots in winter to about three eyes and reduce the main canes by about one third, after which any twiggy wood can be cut away completely. 'Madame Isaac Pereire' and one or two others produce their best flowers on wood of the current season, which means that the autumn crop is often of higher quality than that of midsummer. Pruning does encourage this new wood to form.

## Bourbons

**Adam Messerich**  As this was raised in 1920 it is out of the mainstream of the Bourbons, but it is a good one nevertheless. 6ft × 5ft (1.8 × 1.5m), its first flowers come early in the summer and there is a good second crop, but there are few in between. They are large, little more than semi-double and rather loosely formed, but the warm pink colouring holds well. Can be used as a free-standing shrub, but better still on a pillar. Good foliage, a strong fragrance, and long flower stems for cutting.

**Blairii No. 2**  Blair, 1845. R. *chinensis* × 'Tuscany'. It is reported that Mr Blair's No. 1 seedling is still in cultivation, but I have never seen it, and understand that it is nothing like as good as this one, which would, indeed, take some beating. Probably most easily accommodated as a climber, in which form it will reach 15ft (4.5m) or so, it can also, if you have room, be grown as a large, informal shrub with deep chestnut-red shoots, occupying a space 8ft × 6ft (2.4 × 1.8m). The flowering period in early summer is short, no more than one month, but quite magnificent while it lasts, the blooms appearing along the strong, arching canes. They are large, double, with neatly infolded petals, deep pink in the centre and paling towards the petal edges. Very fragrant. For the best results, carry out the minimum of pruning immediately after flowering. In other words, the best flowers come on well-ripened wood and not on the current season's growth.

**Boule de Neige**  1867. In flower right through the summer, usually making quite a small, erect shrub about 4ft (1.2m) tall and

76

not spreading out a great deal. The small clusters of crimson buds open to 2½in (6cm) rather globular creamy-white blooms, the outer petals of which curve back all round. Occasionally they have a pink flush. There are also short stems bearing individual flowers, so that the blooms are well distributed. Smooth, dark green leaves and a sweet scent. See Pl. 9.

**Bourbon Queen** ('Souvenir de la Princesse de Lamballe') 1835. Not really the best rose to bear the first of these two names, as there are seldom any autumn flowers. In early summer, however, it does put on a grand display on a robust bush of about 5ft × 5ft (1.5 × 1.5m) or up to about double that height if trained on a pillar or wall. The large double flowers open cupped and rather loosely formed, pink with darker veining and paling towards the petal edges. They are very fragrant and set off by handsome, mid-green foliage.

**Champion of the World** 1894. 'Hermosa' × 'Magna Charta'. The raiser (or introducer) of this rose was just asking for trouble in giving it such a grandiose name. Disappointment is almost invited, which is a pity. There is nothing of the overbearing show-off about this variety and it is, in fact, a fairly restrained grower in a generally robust family. With arching shoots and light green leaves, it is unlikely to top 5ft (1.5m), and the medium-sized, double flowers resemble those of 'La Reine Victoria' in their cupped shape, though there is more reflexing of the petals. The colour is light pink, they are scented, and they come in an unending stream throughout the summer and autumn. So perhaps it is a champion after all.

**Coupe d'Hébé** Laffay, 1840. With its very tall, lax and lanky growth this is a pillar rose pure and simple, climbing up to about 7ft (2.1m). Globular, soft pink flowers which hold their colour well and are lighter on the reverse contrast well with attractive pale green leaves. Only one flush of bloom in early summer.

**Commandant Beaurepaire** ('Panachée d'Angers') 1874. One of the most prolific midsummer flowerers of all, but little if anything afterwards. The blooms are borne in large and small clusters on almost every shoot, are cupped but not fully double, and are of a deep pink, splashed and striped with maroon, purple and lighter pink, making a most striking display. They are sweetly scented and grow on a thorny bush some 6ft × 5ft (1.8 × 1.5m) with yellowish-green leaves. It will produce 6ft (1.8m) shoots in the autumn, but these will only bear the odd flower or two – if you are lucky.

**Ferdinand Pichard** Tanne, 1921. Bourbon, Hybrid Perpetual and even a rambler, this rose has appeared under all these headings, though how anyone could put it in the latter class is quite baffling, and as believable as Redouté painting a rose with the spiked leaves of an iris. But whatever group it belongs to, there is certainly quality in its breeding, making it one of the few truly perpetual striped roses. It forms a 4ft × 4ft (1.2 × 1.2m) spreading shrub with medium-sized cupped flowers in small clusters, striped crimson and deeper pink on a pale pink ground. The colourings have great intensity when the blooms are newly opened, but fade a little later on. Generally there will be at least some of them showing from early summer onwards. The matt, yellowish-green leaves have a fresh, lively appearance until, as is possible, mildew strikes.

**Honorine de Brabant** A rampant grower that will certainly need some support, preferably on a wall or tripod as the many canes may be too crowded to be accommodated on a pillar. As a shrub it will reach 6ft × 6ft (1.8 × 1.8m), thick and very bushy, with large, light green foliage and rather loosely formed, not fully double, cupped and quartered blooms. These are of a pale rosy-mauve, spotted and striped a darker mauve and crimson, and they are very fragrant. In many ways they are similar to 'Commandant Beaurepaire' though rather paler, and they do in this case come later in the year as well as in early summer.

**Kathleen Harrop** 1919. This is a sport from the Bourbon climber 'Zéphirine Drouhin', but as it is not quite so vigorous it makes a very pleasing free-standing though lax shrub. It will reach 5ft × 5ft (1.5 × 1.5m) with flowers of a lighter colour than those of its parent, clear pink with a cerise reverse. A pleasing scent, but the second crop of bloom can be disappointing, particularly so if mildew strikes at the same time, which is reasonably likely.

78

**La Reine Victoria** 1872. This is one of the loveliest of the Bourbons, though by no means typical in several ways. It grows to about 5ft (1.5m) but its lax canes need support from a pillar, as I mentioned earlier, on which it can be confined to about 3ft (1m) across, so that it is one of the best for a small garden. The blooms are exquisite, cupped in shape and with paper-thin, shell-like petals of the most delicate pink and a sweet scent. The colour deepens in hot sun, but there can be staining in wet weather and the footstalks of the flowers are rather prone to mildew, which can spread to the leaves if it is not dealt with promptly.

**Louise Odier** Margottin, 1851. This is perhaps a more vigorous grower than 'La Reine Victoria', reaching 6ft × 4ft (1.8 × 1.2m) but with the same slender shoots which are apt to be weighed down by the clustered blooms if they are not tied in to a pillar or tripod. It has similar cupped or goblet-shaped flowers, but the pink this time has more than a hint of lilac about it. Both roses keep almost continuously in flower, though those of the autumn flush are usually smaller than the early ones.

**Madame Ernst Calvat** Schwartz, 1888. A sport from 'Madame Isaac Pereire' (the next on the list) and a tremendous grower with attractive red-tinted young leaves. It will make a 7ft × 5ft (2.1 × 1.5m) shrub which will benefit, not so much from some kind of support, as from something like a tripod to keep it under control. It also makes a good pillar rose, with very large and double blooms, globular in shape, often quartered and with crinkly petals of silvery-peach, deepening in the centre to deep rose-pink and with a darker reverse. Fine scent, and a good autumn show. See Pl. 9.

**Madame Isaac Pereire** Garçon, 1880. Enormously vigorous and with blooms of a size to match, though in the first flush some of them can be malformed for a reason that nobody seems fully to understand. In the autumn, however, they are truly magnificent, probably the most richly scented there are, cupped and very double and sometimes quartered, a deep carmine-pink with a slightly paler reverse. It is a colour that blends well with the other old roses, but needs keeping away from the dazzling modern oranges and reds. I do not wish, however, to give the impression that the first blooming is not worth having. This is far from the case as only a proportion of the blooms may not be up to scratch. The thick, tough canes will produce a 7ft × 6ft (2.1 × 1.8m) shrub, or it can be used as a short climber, well covered with large, handsome leaves, but prone to mildew late on. See Pl. 9.

**Madame Lauriol de Barny** Trouillard, 1868. Large, very fragrant, fully double and quartered flowers of a silvery-pink with just a hint of soft purple. Carried in clusters, these make this one of the loveliest of Bourbons at midsummer, but there will not be more than the odd bloom or two later on. As a shrub it has strong, arching canes, which could perhaps be blessed with a few more leaves. It will reach 5ft × 4ft (1.5 × 1.2m) or can be grown as a pillar rose. Black spot possible.

**Madame Pierre Oger** Oger, introduced by Verdier, 1878. A sport of 'La Reine Victoria' and with it, and 'Louise Odier', makes a trio of similar growth pattern and flower form. Here, the cupped blooms are of a creamy-blush which deepens to a marked degree in hot sunshine. 6ft × 3ft (1.8 × 1m) if kept upright by a pillar, and needing the same tying in as its parent – and the same sharp eye for the first signs of mildew on the footstalks of the flowers and the mid-green, matt leaves, and for black spot.

**Prince Charles** Clusters of 4in (10cm) double flowers in what can best (if inadequately) be described as cerise-maroon, veined crimson-purple, fading after a while to purplish lilac and at all times much paler at the petal bases. Some, though not marked, perfume, and few if any late blooms after the early summer flush. Fine, dark green leaves on a robust plant that will reach 5ft × 4ft (1.5 × 1.2m). Few thorns. Black spot possible.

**Souvenir de la Malmaison** Béluze, 1843. 'Madame Desprez' × a Tea rose. A lusty, bushy grower to about 5ft × 4ft (1.5 × 1.2m) which in my experience (though I have seen this hotly disputed) opens its flowers much more freely if the sun keeps shining. Then it seems to be always in bloom, the large, 5in (13cm) flowers being very full, opening flat and quartered and of the most delicate, creamy blush-pink. Generally healthy, it will go up to 6ft (1.8m) on a pillar, but there is also a climbing form which will considerably exceed this.

**Souvenir de St Anne's** Introduced by Thomas, 1950. Found in a Dublin garden, this is a most un-Bourbon-like sport of 'Souvenir de la Malmaison'. The flowers, of great refinement, are only just semi-double and open to something like 3in (7.5cm) across, the palest blush-pink, deeper on the reverse, and fading almost to white. They are carried in great profusion and fine continuity on an arching, mounding bush that resembles its parent and which will reach 6ft (1.8m) or so after some years.

**Variegata di Bologna** Bonfiglioli, 1909. The flowers of this 6ft × 5ft (1.8 × 1.5m) bush are very double, cupped to globular in shape, with dark crimson-purple striping on a lilac-white ground and full quartering of the petals. Sometimes the odd petal or two in the centre of a flower is purple only, without the striping, and an occasional completely purple bloom indicates a rose of that colour in the ancestry. A memorable first flush and a less dependable second one, though there will certainly be some late bloom. A good, lusty grower, with the single drawback that black spot is almost certain late in the season. Very fragrant. See Pl. 9.

**Zigeuner Knabe** Lambert, 1909. Also known as 'Gipsy Doy', this was a latecomer on the scene and only resembles a Bourbon in its lusty habit, for it will make a bush 7ft × 7ft (2.1 × 2.1m), constantly forming new canes which will reach that length in a single season. I have just been measuring a number that have done so, and this was on a rose grown from a cutting only three years ago. The flowers come in small clusters all along the branches and are about 3in (7.5cm) in diameter, very double and opening flat to give a glimpse of golden stamens. In colour they are of a deep crimson-purple, white at the petal bases, though this cannot be seen until they drop. No scent and once-flowering only. Rather rounded leaves, not unlike those of a Gallica (which I suspect must be in the background somewhere because of the flower form), but they are much healthier. The many thorns give a good handhold for scrambling into other shrubs, which it is well suited to do.

*Portlands*

Because they were infertile as breeders and possibly because the full strength of the large and powerful French nursery trade of the

81

time was behind the swift upsurge in the popularity of the Bourbons, another and not dissimilar group of roses which came into existence in the same period never achieved the acclaim it deserved, and most of those varieties that were put on the market have long since vanished. These were the Portland roses which, though first raised in Italy, possibly from a cross between the 'Autumn Damask' and 'Slater's Crimson China' (though I have heard it said with equal conviction that it may have been the Gallica 'Officinalis'), were named Portland roses after the then Duchess of Portland. Known also as Perpetual Damasks, in most respects they resemble the Bourbons, if not quite so vigorous. Apart from the original Portland rose itself, the few that have survived have big, globular, very double flowers of the Bourbon type and are fully remontant. They form an important link in the chain leading to the Hybrid Perpetuals and hence our modern roses, for they, together with their better-known cousins, were largely used in the creation of the early Hybrid Perpetual varieties. Pruning involves the cutting away of spent and twiggy wood in spring and the trimming back of the longest side shoots.

**Comte de Chambord** 1860. Probably the best of the Portlands now available, this forms a 4ft × 3ft (1.2 × 1m) robust bush that starts to flower in early summer and is seldom without some blooms from then until the frosts set in. They are very double, opening to rather muddled quartering, and are extremely fragrant. The colour is bright pink, paler at the petal edges. See Pl. 8.

**Jacques Cartier** Moreau-Robert, 1868. A shrub with the light green, rather pointed leaves of the group, erect in habit and reaching 4ft × 3ft (1.2 × 1m). The flowers are large, very double and quartered, and of a strong pink, paling almost to white at the edges of the petals. As the flower ages the pink fades considerably and the whole bloom loses its shape. New blooms are, however, coming along the whole time.

**The Portland Rose** (R. *paestana*, 'Duchess of Portland', 'Scarlet Four Seasons') Prior to 1810. This is the original and makes an upright, 4ft × 3ft (1.2 × 1m) bush with bright green leaves and the clusters of flowers well displayed above it, which is certainly more in keeping with a Gallica than a China rose. So also is the flower form, cupped to flat and semi-double with yellow stamens, of a brighter and deeper crimson-pink than 'Officinalis' – though by no means dissimilar except that the blooms repeat in the autumn. Not much scent, but the long, narrow hips take us back to the Damask. See Pl. 8.

## Chapter 10

# Hybrid Perpetuals

ANYONE who makes a categorical statement as to the parentage of the first Hybrid Perpetual is asking for trouble. I know. I once made one before I knew better. There is even a school of thought that maintains that the Hybrid Perpetuals preceded the Bourbons, and though this is difficult to disprove, they are more generally considered to be descended from them through crossings with China roses. The answer is, of course, that new groups of roses do not come into existence overnight. It can take many years, and there is always an overlap between the new and the old. Tracing the history of any early rose family is rather like taking part in a country dance; four steps forward and three steps back. Then you whirl around two or three times with what you think are the facts, hoping all the while that you will both come out at the end of it still in time with the music. Sometimes the founder of a new family was not recognised until some years after its introduction. This was the case with 'La France', the first Hybrid Tea, which was originally classed as a Hybrid Perpetual. Only gradually did people (whirling with abandon) begin to see that nature was producing roses sufficiently different to warrant a new class name. A backwards look was needed to decide which had been the first and 'La France' was decided on, though there were other candidates. All this is reasonably fully documented, which is not the case with the Hybrid Perpetuals. No variety was clearly the first. They crept forward unannounced, but it was the second half of the nineteenth century before they reached their peak of popularity, when there were hundreds of varieties on the market.

In habit of growth and overall size, the Hybrid Perpetuals can, in the most general terms, be said to come halfway between the Bourbons and the Hybrid Teas. However, once again one immediately thinks of how many exceptions there are – the upright and compact 'Mrs John Laing' which is unlikely to go over 5ft (1.5m), the freely branching, bushy 'Reine des Violettes' which will make a sizeable shrub in the right soil, and 'Hugh Dickson' which unless tied or pegged down will wave its 7–8ft (2.1–2.4m) canes about in the wind like the tentacles of an octopus, bearing flowers only at the tips.

The blooms of Hybrid Perpetuals much resemble those of the Bourbons – large, cabbagy and full of petals. They were given the name they bear because by the standards of their time that is what they were. But they are not anything like perpetual. The majority flower profusely in early summer before resting for a number of weeks. The quality and quantity of the second blooming can vary with the same variety from year to year, while with others there is no repeat at all, which should not be forgotten when making a choice of those to buy.

Many Hybrid Perpetuals will make fine specimen shrubs, or they can be planted in groups of three or four, either of one kind or mixed, as the colours of all of them blend well together. As distinct from many of the other old varieties, the petals have one, unshaded colour only, either white, crimson, maroon, various pinks or purple. Three notable exceptions to this are 'Baron Girod de l'Ain', the very similar 'Roger Lambelin' – the petal edges of both of which are white edged and flecked and also scalloped – and 'Reine des Violettes', which has flat, quartered Gallica-like flowers that pass through many shades of maroon and purple and violet-grey before the petals drop.

All thrive especially in a coolish climate. Black spot and mildew may make an appearance, but like so many of the old roses they seem able to discount it and there are no permanent ill effects. Prune to three or four buds the first spring after planting, and unless you intend to peg them down (see page 165) follow the pattern that was outlined for the Bourbons.

**Baron Girod de l'Ain** Reverchon, 1897. A sport of 'Eugéne Fürst'. The large, double, fragrant, deep crimson-red blooms of this rose open cupped and with, as I said above, the petal edges irregularly scalloped and flecked with white. It is a robust grower to 5ft × 3ft (1.5 × 1m) and a fairly healthy one, and even if the flowers do lose some of their sparkle as they age and the red dulls, they are still a talking point in any collection of old roses. Fully remontant. Large, deep green leaves. Compare with 'Roger Lambelin' below.

**Baronne Prévost** Desprez, 1842. One of the earliest of the Hybrid Perpetuals, but never surpassed in the beauty of its clusters of large, double, clear rose-pink blooms, which open out to show a button eye. Each is about 4in (10cm) across and fragrant. The bush is sturdy and upright, about 4ft × 3ft (1.2 × 1m), well covered with mid-green leaves, and the continuity of flowering is good.

**Frau Karl Druschki** ('Snow Queen') Lambert, 1901. 'Merveille de Lyon' × 'Madame Caroline Testout'. This is one of the borderline cases that is sometimes classed as a Hybrid Tea, but in appearance and habit it is much more of a Hybrid Perpetual. It rests from flowering in the middle of the summer as they do, and it is tall and lanky as so many of them are. The blooms are double and quite shapely, sometimes streaked with pink in the bud but showing no sign of it when they open to the purest white, but unfortunately they are completely scentless. Most of them come in clusters at the ends of the main canes, and as they are very close together some disbudding will allow those that are left to develop to their peak of beauty, when they will be very large indeed. A vigorous grower to 5ft (1.5m) or so, the longer canes can be pegged down effectively. Light green, matt foliage, by no means unattractive to mildew spores.

**Général Jacqueminot** Roussel, 1853. Possibly a seedling of 'Gloire des Rosomanes'. Introduced by a French amateur, this one has the most wonderful scarlet-crimson double flowers and is one of the forebears of such roses as 'Crimson Glory' and 'Ena Harkness'. There are, in fact, well over five hundred roses descended from it, and it was so popular as a breeding rose that it acquired the accolade of a nickname, General Jack – unless, of course, it was that understandably nobody felt like attempting to pronounce its real name. It has the long centre petals of the later Hybrid Perpetuals, so that the blooms are reasonably high-centred at first, though they do open out more fully later, at all times beautifully scented. The 4ft × 3ft (1.2 × 1m) bush puts on a tremendous display at midsummer, but is not quite so free-flowering in the autumn, when some mildew may be present. Better than many of the family in hot weather. See Pl. 10.

**Georg Arends** Hinner, 1910. As a latecomer, it has the scrolled, pointed bud, developing into a high-centred flower, that one associates with modern roses. The colour is of the most lovely transparent rose-pink with a touch of cream on the reverse of the petals and a sweet scent. It tends to go up rather more than it should for shapeliness, to something approaching 6ft (1.8m) without spreading out much. A candidate for pegging, clearly. Light green leaves.

**George Dickson** Dickson, 1912. A strong grower up to 5ft (1.5m), it has large, cupped blooms of deep crimson-purple with a wonderful scent. Its main weakness is in the flower stems so that the blooms nod, but they are high enough up as a rule to be appreciated by anyone free from lumbago. In my earlier book I included 'Hugh Dickson', stablemate of 'George', in the list of recommendations. I now feel this was a mistake, for which I hope to be forgiven by anyone who has bought it on my advice. There is nothing wrong with the rich crimson flowers, but there certainly is with the way in which they are displayed, waving about at the tips of immensely long canes, and in a wind looking as if they were holding on for dear life. Pegging down will certainly help, but there are much better roses to spend your money on.

**Mrs John Laing** Bennett, 1887. 'François Michelon' seedling. A stiff, upright-growing rose that has been a great favourite since its introduction nearly one hundred years ago. The 4½in (11.5cm) flowers are very full, globular in form, and of a bright silvery rose-pink with a hint of lilac in it. It is probably the most free-flowering of all the Hybrid Perpetuals and is very remontant, little bothered by rain or the damp autumn air. It keeps compact, reaching only 5ft × 3ft (1.5 × 1m) on average. Sweet scent and healthy, light green, rather small leaves.

**Paul Neyron** Levet, 1869. 'Victor Verdier' × 'Anna de Diesbach'. Strong upright canes will take this rose to 5–6ft (1.5–1.8m), but despite its height it is generally self-supporting. The blooms, mostly coming in clusters, are truly spectacular, fully 5in (13cm) across, double and opening wide, though there is some lack of discipline in the way the petals arrange themselves. They are deep rose-pink and somewhat lighter on the reverse. Very little scent, unfortunately, but it takes no more than four or five of the flowers to fill a vase that will become the focal point of any room it graces and will last well. Handsome, shiny foliage and a good repeat in the autumn after a short breather in late summer. See Pl. 10.

**Prince Camille de Rohan** ('La Rosière') Verdier, 1861. Possibly 'Général Jacqueminot' × 'Géant des Batailles'. A romantic name and a dramatic flower in keeping with it. Only of medium size, the blooms are double, shapely and of a velvety blackish crimson, with hints of maroon and purple. As a plant it is one of the less vigorous of the family, rarely exceeding 4ft (1.2m) in height, and after the midsummer flush it can be shy in starting again. More than most it needs a cool season to give its best, but the blooms do not seem to mind rain and are richly scented. Very liable to mildew, and can be affected by rust. The flowers, however, overcome my reservations in putting it forward.

**Reine des Violettes** Millet-Malet, 1860. 'Pius IX' seedling. As its name would suggest, the sumptuous, double, quartered blooms are violet-purple when fully expanded, a strong earlier hint of cerise quickly vanishing. The greyish-green leaves form a perfect foil for the flowers and come on a big, 6ft (1.8m), spreading and freely branching bush which needs good soil to thrive. Otherwise it can be rather short-lived. Fairly hard pruning in early spring is also a good idea, and if well looked after this can be one of the most rewarding and continuous-flowering of all the Hybrid Perpetuals. The only problem is that it does not look in the least like one. The flowers resemble a Gallica, and the bush one of the less upright Bourbons. See Pl. 10.

**Roger Lambelin** Schwartz, 1890. A sport of 'Fisher Holmes'. This has been mentioned when discussing 'Baron Girod de l'Ain' as the flowers of both have the strange characteristic of white edging to the scalloped dark red petals. This is the smaller of the two, both in its flowers, which open out and reflex rather more, and in its size as a bush. I have not, however, found the lack of vigour that is often attributed to it, though to be on the safe side I do keep it well fed. With me it reaches 4ft × 3ft (1.2 × 1m), fairly open in habit but branching well, and with light green leaves which are not immune to disease. The strongly scented flowers
88

hold their colour better than those of 'Baron Girod de l'Ain', the dusky crimson-red being undimmed by time. Good repeat. See Pl. 10.

**Souvenir du Docteur Jamain** Lacharme, 1865. A 'Charles Lefèbvre' seedling. The rich wine-red double flowers are unexcelled provided the weather is on the cool side, but a hot sun over several hours can make them look a little dingy and spoil the colour. They are very fragrant and if planted where the full heat of the midday sun is kept from them are singularly lovely. Growing it on a west wall is one way of doing this, when it will go up to 8–9ft (2.4–2.7m). As a free-standing shrub it will be at least 3ft (1m) less.

**Vick's Caprice** 1897. Discovered by J. Vick in America, and possibly a sport from 'Archiduchesse Elisabeth d'Autriche'. The high-centred blooms here show Tea rose influence, the deep pink buds opening soft pink, splashed and striped white and a stronger pink. They grow on a compact bush which is unlikely to go beyond 4ft × 3ft (1.2 × 1m). Fully remontant, this is a fine and very decorative rose, with only a dislike of rain to mar its good qualities. Wet weather and it hangs its head in shame at the condition of its petals, but then it does not rain every day.

*Chapter 11*

# The Rugosas

ALTHOUGH the original Rugosas go back into the mists of time in China and Japan – they can be seen in old prints and paintings from both countries – they were not considered of much attraction when they eventually arrived in the West, being leggy and spindly and having flowers which did not last when cut for the house. It was not until the end of the last century and the beginning of this one that practically all the hybrids we grow today were raised, and they turned out to be some of the very best flowering shrubs there are. The one qualification to this is that, with very few exceptions such as the Grootendorst hybrids, they do not make good cut flowers.

However, their assets are legion, with fresh green foliage that appears very early in the year and is quite disease-proof. Coupled with this are continuous bloom throughout the summer and autumn and, on the single and semi-double varieties, enormous scarlet hips.

The leaves are particularly distinct, being deeply ribbed (rugose) which gives them a crinkled appearance found in no other roses. Rugosas will grow in almost any soil, make good seaside shrubs and are ideal for hedges, being clothed with leaves right down to the ground and quite impenetrable, for they are all incredibly prickly. Tackling a Rugosa with secateurs can be like pruning a wasps' nest.

When used in hedges they will stand a certain amount of gentle clipping over in winter to keep them in shape, but otherwise they fortunately require little pruning except the tipping back of new growths and the occasional removal of an odd spent branch or two. Some removal of old flower heads, at least after the first flush of bloom early in the summer, will help to keep the flowers coming, but even without this they will still put on a good and

90

continuous show. With those that produce hips, you will not, of course, have so many of these, at any rate early on, if you carry out dead-heading. The flowers shed their petals cleanly and never look, as some sodden rose blooms do, like something the police have recovered with a grappling hook from a river. The hips of Rugosas are, incidentally, very rich in vitamin C and make good rosehip syrup and jam.

The colours of the group range from the purest white of 'Blanc Double de Coubert', through the pink of 'Fru Dagmar Hastrup', to the deep wine-red of 'Roseraie de l'Hay'; there is one comparatively modern hybrid, 'Agnes', which is yellow. 'Max Graf', a hybrid with a rambler, grows prostrate along the ground and is useful for covering waste areas.

Those I have mentioned, with the exception of 'Max Graf', the majority of hybrids in fact, have a distinct family resemblance to the original Rugosa in the flowers, leaves and very spiny stems. There are a few, however, represented by 'Conrad Ferdinand Meyer' and its sport 'Nova Zembla', and including rather less markedly so 'Sarah Van Fleet', that have growth and flowers more closely resembling those of the less double and more loosely formed Bourbons. These have conventional thorns – though still plenty of them – and less healthy and less distinctive leaves. But even allowing for this they are still a match for most roses, coming into bloom early and being unbeatable for continuity. They have their place in the garden just as much as the other Rugosas and their own particular part to play.

**Agnes** Saunders, 1900. R. *rugosa* × R. *foetida persiana*. This came to Britain from Canada, and apart from being that oddity a yellow Rugosa it lacks some of the quality of most of the others. It flowers in early summer but the blooms are rather short-lived and it is not as remontant as it might be. They are about 3in (7.5cm) in diameter, forming fully double pompons of pale amber-yellow, shading to cream at the petal edges and with a sweet scent. The bush is tall, probably up to 7ft (2.1m), but it is not particularly dense-growing and can look straggly. Very good, bright green leaves, however.

There is, in fact, one other more or less yellow Rugosa, though the yellow has pink flushes. It is called 'Dr Eckener', the long canes of which are particularly viciously thorned and very wide-spreading and unpredictable in their direction, so that this rose is only suitable for somebody who wants to have the complete Rugosa range and who is justified, by virtue of its size, in calling their garden 'grounds', or even a demesne.

**Alba** This makes a dense, spreading bush, ideal as a wide screening or hedging shrub, provided you have space for something that will reach 6ft × 6ft (1.8 × 1.8m) and look fairly solid with it. It comes into flower at midsummer, its single blooms white with delicate veining on the petals and with golden anthers. They come in clusters, with blush-pink buds, and the flowers are followed by a fine show of orange-red, tomato-shaped hips of considerable size. These blend well with the later flowers and with the rich gold of the foliage as it assumes its autumn tints. See Pl. 13.

**Belle Poitevine** Bruant, 1894. This would make a more restrained hedge or screen, for which it is very suitable, as it only grows to some 5ft (1.5m) and spreads out to about the same distance if left alone. The large semi-double flowers are shapely at first but open rather loosely formed, though basically flat; they are purplish-pink in colour and have creamy stamens. Not a great deal of scent and usually only a few hips.

**Blanc Double de Coubert** Cochet-Cochet, 1892. R. *rugosa* × 'Sombreuil'. From the French raiser of some of the best hybrids we have, and well up to standard. It forms a 6ft × 5ft (1.8 × 1.5m) shrub, more open, particularly at the base, than some of the others and with typical, fresh green foliage completely free from disease. The 4in (10cm) flowers are informal, very sweetly scented and of the purest papery-white imaginable, set off by buff anthers. They are not particularly rain-proof, but they come with such freedom that the spoiling of a few does not matter too much. The only problem may be that sodden petals in the closely packed clusters may drape themselves over opening buds, which does not do them a lot of good. The hips that form do not, in my experience, pass beyond the small, green stage and then wither away. AM 1895.

**Conrad Ferdinand Meyer** Müller, 1899. A Rugosa hybrid × 'Gloire de Dijon'. A formidable name for a formidable rose, for it will soar to 8–10ft (2.4–3m), bristling with fierce thorns on canes singularly lacking in leaves or laterals lower down. Hard pruning does not seem to help much and is something that needs both courage and leather gloves to tackle, but grow this rose behind other shrubs and it can be seen in all its true beauty. It is very early into bloom with a truly breathtaking crop of 4½in (11.5cm) silvery-pink double flowers, shapely at first before they open wide. This show goes on and on, slackens for a short while, and comes yet again. Glossy, dark, leathery foliage is in keeping but is subject to black spot and, in some areas, to rust. Unless strong and rigid support is given it will be difficult to keep the long, flower-crowned canes under control and when they rub against each other in the wind the thorns can cause considerable damage. A tripod would be a better answer than a pillar because there is more of it to tie the rose in to. AM 1901.

**Fimbriata** ('Dianthiflora', 'Phoebe's Frilled Pink') Morlet, 1891. *R. rugosa* × 'Madame Alfred Carrière'. A Noisette climber crossed with a Rugosa could hardly be expected to produce a rose with flowers with petal edges serrated like a dianthus. The Grootendorst group have the same feature, equally inexplicably, but they came considerably later than 'Fimbriata' and there is nothing about any of the other Rugosas to give a pointer as to why these few should be different. Anyway, whatever the answer, this is a beautiful and refined little rose, its soft pink flowers larger and opening wider than those of 'Pink Grootendorst', with which it has been compared. To me they are much more refined, and they are also scented, but it must be said that they do not come with quite the same freedom. A 5ft × 4ft (1.5 × 1.2m) bush, upright and fairly sturdy. AM 1896. See Pl. 13.

**F.J. Grootendorst** de Goey, introduced by Grootendorst, 1918. *R. rugosa rubra* × an unknown Polyantha. This can form a very tall and untypically open bush up to 8ft × 6ft (2.4 × 1.8m), but it may be kept at least two feet lower by pruning and does not seem to suffer any ill effects. The clusters of scentless flowers, which come with great freedom and continuity from early summer onwards, are of a rich crimson, small individually, but there are often upwards of twenty per spray. The entry for 'Fimbriata' above has already made clear that 'F.J. Grootendorst' has serrated petal edges. There is also healthy, Rugosa-type foliage, though on the small side. No hips form so no dead-heading is needed.

**Fru Dagmar Hastrup** (Frau Dagmar Hartopp) Nobody knows where it comes from or when, and nobody seems certain which of its two names is the right one. A slightly pathetic state of affairs, but whatever name you buy this rose under it will repay you, if only because it is one of the smaller and more compact Rugosas. If you have been worried about finding space for any of them then here is the one for you, for this rose will not go over 4–5ft (1.2–1.5m) and will be rather less across, making it an excellent choice for a low hedge. It starts into flower early and has particularly lovely and very large single pale pink blooms which are delicately veined on the petals and have cream stamens. It is a wonderful blend of soft colours and the blooms are followed by the finest hips of all the family, round and rich crimson. The usual good and healthy foliage. AM 1958, AGM 1958. See Pl. 13.

**Max Graf** Bowditch, 1919. Probably R. *rugosa* × R. *wichuraiana*. Most roses of slightly doubtful parentage are classed with the family they most resemble, but this is not the case here. A hybrid of a Rugosa with a rambler, it looks and behaves much more like the latter in that it spreads naturally along the ground as R. *wichuraiana* will do, though it can be trained upwards. There are plenty of other roses for that, however. The leaves resemble those of a rambler and are smooth and glossy. In time they will make a fairly thick carpet and keep down weeds, but not, it must be said, those that flourish in the winter months when the rose's leaves have gone. Plentiful clusters of 2in (5cm) single pink flowers, which pale to white at the base of the petals and have golden stamens, appear all along the sprawling canes rather later than most roses and last for a considerable period, though there is no repeat. Best suited for hiding an unsightly bank where it can ramble at will, rooting as it goes where it touches the ground. AM 1964.

**Nova Zembla** Introduced by Mees, 1907. A 'Conrad Ferdinand Meyer' sport. Apart from its white flowers in place of the pink, and a slightly less daunting habit of growth, this closely resembles the parent.

94

**Pink Grootendorst** Grootendorst, 1923. If you want to ask for this from a Dutch nursery, do not pronounce Grootendorst as it is spelt. I once did this when discussing it with a Dutchman and he had not the slightest idea what I was talking about. On the other hand, do not ask me what it should be. The pronunciation did not come easily to an English tongue or ear, was mastered one minute and forgotten the next. But be that as it may, this is a sport from 'F.J. Grootendorst' dating from 1923, very similar if slightly less vigorous, and with bright pink flowers which to my mind are more attractive. Occasionally an odd branch will revert to the dark red of the parent. Alone of the Rugosas this subfamily make roses that are good for cutting and that last well in a vase. There is, I believe, a 'White Grootendorst', but I have not seen it. AM 1953. See Pl. 13.

**Rose à Parfum de l'Hay** Gravereaux, 1901. (R. × *damascena* × 'Général Jacqueminot') × R. *rugosa*. This appears to be definitely a rose for a warm climate, where it will grow into a substantial bush of 5 ft × 5 ft (1.5 × 1.5 m) as against not more than 4ft (1.2m) in areas of cold winters and wettish summers. Nodding, double, mauve-crimson flowers which, in view of the name chosen for the rose, should have a rich scent but quite simply do not. There is some, but not much, and it may be wondered at this stage why I have included a variety that hardly sounds a world-beater in comparison with the other Rugosas. But friends abroad, in California for instance, have raved about it, so if you live in what you think might be the right place, give it a try. After all, it has been in cultivation for over eighty years, so somebody must love it.

**Roseraie de l'Hay** Cochet-Cochet, 1901. An R. *rugosa rosea* sport. Without doubt one of the finest Rugosas of all, but you must have room for it, for given time it will achieve 8ft × 8ft (2.4 × 2.4m), densely clothed right to the ground with healthy, bright green foliage on which disease is unknown. The clusters of flowers, halfway between semi-double and double, begin to appear very early in the summer or even in late spring, and from that time on never stop coming until the onset of winter at last puts an end to them. They are of very rich, velvety wine-red, really sumptuous and beautifully scented, but there will be no hips. Wonderful for a hedge and it will not resent some pruning to keep it a little less massive. See Pl. 13.

**Rubra**   Vigorous and more lax in habit than most of this family, it builds to a fine bushy plant about 5ft × 5ft (1.5 × 1.5m), well covered with leaves. Scarlet hips follow the clusters of single, deep pink flowers with their cream stamens. See Pl. 13

**Sarah Van Fleet**   Van Fleet, 1926. Possibly R. *rugosa* × 'My Maryland'. Not unlike 'Conrad Ferdinand Meyer' in its habit of growth, but it is certainly more bushy and I would say more lax as well. It mixes very well with other plants, or if spaced about 3ft (1m) apart will make a first-rate hedge, for which it should be pruned to about 4ft (1.2m). The fine clusters of bloom come early in the year, each flower rather more than semi-double, cupped but somewhat loosely formed, warm rose-pink and with creamy stamens. A fine, healthy rose that will tolerate some shade. AM 1962.

**Scabrosa**   Its identity lost in the mists of time, this one was reintroduced to the market by the Harkness nurseries who had grown it for many years. Its name may even now be wrong according to Jack Harkness, and certainly does not convey the attractions of what is one of the best of the Rugosas. It has the largest flowers of any of them, some 4–5in (10–13cm) in diameter, single and with delicate-looking petals of a soft fuchsia-pink and yellow stamens. One of the first into bloom each year, it has particularly good foliage and huge tomato-red hips. Will reach 6ft (1.8m).

**Schneezwerg** ('Snowdwarf')   Lambert, 1912. R. *rugosa* × a Polyantha? From late spring this rose is rarely out of flower, the 2½in (7cm) blooms resembling those of a Japanese anemone, semi-double, opening flat, white, and with a boss of golden stamens. They come in clusters of varying size and cover a shrub that is dense, twiggy and shapely, about 4ft × 5ft (1.2 × 1.5m) and with plenty of small glossy leaves. Its spreading habit makes it fine for a hedge, as the branches of one will intertwine with its neighbours and make a very thick screen. Good scent and reasonable weather resistance, any damaged blooms being replaced almost before they are gone. The small orange hips are quite showy. AM 1948.

**Souvenir de Philémon Cochet**   Cochet-Cochet, 1899. A sport of 'Blanc Double de Coubert'. In most ways a duplicate of its parent
96

Four roses very important historically. The 'Autumn Damask' (*top left*), accidentally crossed with 'Old Blush' (*top right*), a China rose, gave remontant garden roses to the West. *Bottom left*, R. *gallica* 'Officinalis', the earliest cultivated rose we know. *Bottom right*, R. *foetida persiana* gave us our yellow garden roses.

PLATE 1

'Nevada' is one of the best and most spectacular for specimen planting.

R. × *paulii rosea*, low-growing but wide-spreading for ground cover.

R. *moyesii* 'Geranium', the best of this family for the smaller garden.

R. × *highdownensis* has hips typical of the Moyesii family.

R. *rubrifolia*, showing the display of hips and the blue-green leaves.

The hips of the Apple Rose, R. *pomifera*, do not much resemble apples.

*PLATE* 2

R. *spinosissima bicolor* is one of the many small Scotch roses.

'Stanwell Perpetual', the only Spinosissima to keep flowering.

'Frühlingsmorgen', perhaps the loveliest of the Kordes hybrids.

PLATE 3

'Charles de Mills' is a typical Gallica in habit, but with unique flowers.

'Complicata'. A very untypical rambling Gallica hybrid.

'Empress Josephine', a lax, spreading Gallica for foreground planting.

'Perle des Panachées', one of the many striped Gallicas.

'Ispahan' has perhaps the longest flowering season of all Damasks.

'La Ville de Bruxelles', a Damask that holds its colour exceptionally well.

PLATE 4

One of the oldest and largest of the Damasks is 'Trigintipetala'.

The green eye is a distinctive feature of the flowers of the Damask 'Madame Hardy'.

Pink flecks on the petal edges mean 'Leda' is also the 'Painted Damask'.

R. × *alba semi-plena* dates back perhaps to Roman times.

PLATE 5

'Félicité Parmentier' is probably the best Alba for the small garden.

'Königin von Danemarck' is another Alba of reasonable size.

The Alba 'Celestial' is also known as 'Céleste', and is one of the loveliest.

'Chapeau de Napoléon' is a Centifolia, despite the mossy calyces.

PLATE 6

'De Meaux' is a dwarf Centifolia suitable for foreground planting.

The brightest red among the Moss roses is found in 'Henri Martin'.

'Fantin-Latour', one of the most upright-growing of the Centifolias.

'William Lobb', a tall Moss rose that needs a pillar or wall.

'Gloire des Mousseux' has probably the biggest flowers of all Moss roses.

'Péllison' is quite a bushy grower for a Moss rose.

PLATE 7

'Madame Laurette Messimy', a low-growing, free-flowering China rose.

'Hermosa', a small, neat China, can be used for bedding.

*R. chinensis mutabilis*, unique in colouring, makes a shrub or short climber.

One of the few Portland roses still in cultivation is 'Comte de Chambord'.

*R. chinensis* 'Major', also called *R. indica* 'Major' when used as a rootstock.

'The Portland Rose' or 'Scarlet Four Seasons'.

*PLATE 8*

'Madame Isaac Pereire' (Bourbon) is one of the most fragrant of roses.

'Variegata di Bologna', a striped Bourbon of great distinction.

'Madame Ernst Calvat', a sport of 'Madame Isaac Pereire' and equally good.

'Boule de Neige', upright and less vigorous than many Bourbons.

PLATE 9

The Hybrid Perpetual 'Général Jacqueminot', ancestor of many modern red roses.

'Paul Neyron' has the most sumptuous flowers of all the Hybrid Perpetuals.

'Reine des Violettes', a Hybrid Perpetual with the flowers of a Gallica.

The Hybrid Perpetual 'Roger Lambelin', showing the effect of pegging down.

'The Fairy', a low-growing rambler sport.

'Cécile Brunner' is a Tea-Polyantha, here shown in climbing form.

PLATE 10

'Aloha'. Shown here as a climber, but
equally good as a shrub.

'Frühlingsgold' is ideal for a large
specimen planting.

'Erfurt', one of the many fine shrubs
raised by Wilhelm Kordes.

'Angelina', a modern variety that makes a
fine bushy shrub. Not too tall.

A real dazzler, 'First Choice' is a
Floribunda shrub.

'Joseph's Coat' makes a shrub, as here, or
a short climber.

PLATE 11

'Golden Wings' is a really remontant and
not too big shrub.

'Lavender Lassie' has flowers in the old
style in huge trusses.

'Fritz Nobis', a modern shrub rose hybrid
that grows like a wild rose.

'Eye Paint'. Bushy and not too big, it has
flowers that seem to look at you.

PLATE 12

'Pink Grootendorst' is one of the Rugosas that has frilled petals.

Probably the best Rugosa for a hedge is 'Roseraie de l'Hay'.

*R. rugosa rubra* is one of those with single flowers and fine hips.

The Rugosa 'Fimbriata' blending its soft colourings with columbines.

'Fru Dagmar Hastrup' is the ideal Rugosa for a small garden.

*R. rugosa alba*, showing the typical hips of the family.

PLATE *13*

'Ballerina', a small-flowered Hybrid
Musk ideal for a low hedge.

'Cornelia' is one of the Hybrid Musks to
choose for a taller hedge.

'Vanity' brings a pleasing change of
colour to the Hybrid Musks.

'Moonlight', one of the Hybrid Musks
that grows really tall.

'Penelope' is probably the finest of the
Hybrid Musks.

'Magenta' is a rose that must have support
from a stake.

PLATE 14

'Rambling Rector' tree-climbing in the Rose Society's gardens.

The vigorous 'Albertine', shown here as a free-standing shrub.

Almost evergreen foliage is one asset of the rambler 'Félicité et Perpétue'.

'Seagull' is a good rambler for growing on a pergola, as shown here.

PLATE 15

Classed as a Noisette climber, 'Madame
Alfred Carrière' is hardly typical.

'Cl. Mrs Herbert Stevens' (*top*) and
'Cl. Lady Hillingdon', remontant Tea roses.

Once-flowering and with great profusion
sums up 'Madame Grégoire Staechelin'.

A climber or a shrub, 'Sombreuil' is a Tea
rose with flowers in the early style.

'Paul's Lemon Pillar' is really creamy-
white. Not remontant, but very profuse.

'Golden Showers' is equally good as a
shrub or climber.

PLATE *16*

except that the flowers, again pure white, are larger, much more double and less loosely formed, and sometimes there is a blush tint to the closely packed centre petals. Not a rose one sees about much, and more's the pity. The Cochets knew what they were doing around the turn of the century.

## Chapter 12

# The Hybrid Musks

ALL the Hybrid Musks go back to a German rose called 'Trier', but the best-known ones, beginning in 1912 with 'Daphne', were produced by the Rev. Joseph Pemberton by crossing, in the early stages at least, various Hybrid Teas with 'Trier'. He must take responsibility for the misleading name the group bears, for they have only the most distant link with the Musk rose and all most of them have in common with it is their very sweet scent. They do, however, make some of the best flowering shrubs there are, vigorous, remontant, reasonably healthy and ranging in size from the 3–4ft (1–1.2m) 'Danaë' to the 8–9ft (2.4–2.7m) 'Vanity'. The sheer mass of flowers in the first flush is staggering, but a certain amount of dead-heading has to be done – a daunting task with the big ones – if anything like the same display is to be achieved later in the year. Otherwise there will always be a reasonable show of late flowers (and invariably some in between), while some of the many varieties, of which 'Penelope' is probably the best-known example, often send up enormously strong and long canes with huge trusses of bloom in the early autumn months. While spectacular, these can sometimes be given only a qualified welcome, particularly if the shrub is near a path, as they come in the most unexpected places and often at awkward angles. Encroaching on a narrow path on a wet morning they can be anything but welcome – all of which indicates that the Hybrid Musks, or at any rate the bigger ones, should be allowed plenty of space. If they are to be used for a flowering hedge, for which purpose they are unbeatable, be prepared for one that will be 4–5ft (1.2–1.5m) wide at the very least.

It is sometimes said that whatever colour these roses start out, they end up fading to white – always with the honourable exceptions of 'Pax' and 'Moonlight' which are white to start with. With a number of the paler-coloured ones there is some truth in this because they do fade, but it is an exaggeration. And nobody could apply it to the later non-Pemberton developments such as the crimson 'Wilhelm' (which came from Germany) and scarlet 'Will Scarlet', for the Hybrid Musk story is a continuing one. It did not stop with Pemberton and in fact one of his gardeners, J.A. Bentall, put a number of varieties on the market after Pemberton's death. However, it seems likely that these were at least in part the work of the originator of the group, and if so they show an interesting change of direction. A number of them, and one can cite 'Belinda' and more especially 'Ballerina', had much smaller flowers than those that had gone before. Or was it a step backwards to something that had been lying dormant in the Hybrid Musk strain? For at about the same time, the 1930s, Peter Lambert in Germany, who was the original raiser of 'Trier', independently put on the market a rose called 'Mozart' which closely resembled 'Ballerina', though the pink was deeper. Of such are the complexities of rose ancestry.

But back to fact. In general the Hybrid Musks will prosper with the minimum of pruning (dead-heading will do all that is needed), but the unpredictability of growth already mentioned in connection with 'Penelope' is not confined to that rose alone. Some fairly drastic treatment may be needed now and then to keep a semblance of balanced growth. To restrict overall size, no harm will come if all the side shoots are shortened by about two thirds in spring and some of the main canes by approximately one third. And as always with shrub roses, remove completely dead wood as soon as it is seen.

Hedges, specimen shrubs, in a mixed planting, and even with some of the smaller ones, bedding – all these are uses to which Hybrid Musks can be put.

**Ballerina** Bentall, 1937. Unknown parents. A short, 3–4ft (1–1.2m) grower, the many canes forming it into a mound, covered with huge heads of small, dainty, single pink flowers, lightening almost to white at the centre. Not a noticeable scent, but one of the most continuously in flower and with good weather resistance. Fine for a low hedge or the front of a border, or it makes an excellent standard rose with a large, balanced head. See Pl. 14.

**Belinda** Bentall, 1936. Very large trusses of small flowers in a fairly strong pink and fragrant, too. Long, strong, upright canes

99

make this a good hedging rose which will reach about 5ft (1.5m). For some reason not very often listed by nurseries, but then neither, until comparatively recently, was that other Bentall introduction 'Ballerina', which has now become a top favourite. It is up to gardeners to create the same demand for this one. They should.

**Buff Beauty** 1939. Since this is such a recent rose it seems strange that where it comes from is unknown, but that is nevertheless the case. Large clusters of creamy-coloured 2–3in (5–7.5cm) blooms, shapely at first but opening more loosely, scented and double and appearing early in the season. The later blooms take on deep apricot-yellow tones, paling slightly towards the petal edges. Spreading, arching and in other words rather lax in habit, it will in time make a 6ft × 7ft (1.8 × 2.1m) bush with dark, reddish-green stems and purple-tinted foliage. Good continuity of bloom. It can be used as a pillar rose. AGM.

**Cornelia** Pemberton, 1925. With 'Penelope', possibly the best-known of the Hybrid Musks, and almost always in flower from early summer onwards. The salmon-pink buds, in large and small trusses, open to rosette-type blooms of strawberry-pink, flushed yellow, which fade, no, not to white, but to coppery-pink. Glossy, dark green leaves on a fragrant, wide-spreading bush of about 6ft × 7ft (1.8 × 2.1m). If kept compact by pruning, it will make a good hedge. Does not mind rain. See Pl. 14.

**Danaë** Pemberton, 1913. Thought to be 'Trier' × 'Gloire de Chédane-Guinoisseau' and one of the first of the Pemberton introductions. It is also one of the more compact ones, reaching about 4ft × 3ft (1.2 × 1m), but there is no lack of trusses of semi-double, apricot-yellow flowers which fade in time to ivory. Dark green, glossy leaves and a possible candidate for bedding. AM 1912.

**Felicia** Pemberton, 1928. 'Trier' × 'Ophelia'. Lower-growing and even more spreading than most (though not as small as 'Danaë') but still reasonably bushy, it will reach 5ft (1.5m), good for a hedge or for bedding if suitably pruned. Large clusters of 3in (7.5cm) shapely blooms in two tones, china- and salmon-pink, the colour deepening in the centre of the flower. Strong fragrance, and especially good in the autumn. AGM 1965.

**Francesca** Pemberton, 1922. 'Danaë' × 'Sunburst'. Another of those not, for some reason, frequently listed. Dark red wood and fine glossy foliage on a 6ft × 6ft (1.8 × 1.8m) bush, bearing long, apricot-yellow buds which open to rather loosely shaped flowers of the same colour, fading to cream. Good scent.

**Hamburg** Kordes, 1935. 'Eva' × 'Daily Mail Scented Rose'. One of the more modern Hybrid Musks, not of the Pemberton group, and in habit more like a Floribunda. It starts into flower at midsummer with large trusses of semi-double crimson-scarlet blooms, contrasting vividly with the yellow stamens. Rather scanty foliage low down and it does not spread out much below 3ft (1m), so it is best grown at the back of the border. Only a slight scent. 6ft × 3–4ft (1.8 × 1–1.2m).

**Magenta** Kordes, 1954. Yellow Floribunda × 'Lavender Pinocchio'. Another one that does not look like a Hybrid Musk at all, and the classification is suspect. It has 4ft (1.2m), lax canes with clusters of flowers coming mainly at or near the ends and weighing them down to the ground if they are not given some support. However, the flowers themselves are lovely, strongly scented and very double, opening flat and occasionally quartered like the old roses. They are in the most delicate tones of rosy-lilac and mauve-pink, so that the name of the rose is, to say the least, inappropriate. Rather tight clusters mean that the petals of spent blooms do not always fall as cleanly as they should and after rain some attention is necessary if the remaining buds are to open properly. Fairly sparse, dark green foliage on which black spot is always a possibility. A curate's egg. See Pl. 14.

**Moonlight** Pemberton, 1913. 'Trier' × 'Sulphurea', the latter a Tea rose by William Paul in 1900. Lemon-yellow in the bud, the semi-double flowers come in enormous trusses on which I have counted up to eighty flowers, especially in the autumn. They are ivory-white, fading to pure white, and have yellow stamens and a rich fragrance. The dark red canes with their dark green leaves make a robust and bushy grower of about 4–5ft (1.2–1.5m). AM 1913. See Pl. 14.

**Nur Mahal** Pemberton, 1923. 'Château de Clos Vougeot' × a Hybrid Musk seedling. Perhaps this is in fewer gardens than any of the other Pemberton roses, and yet it is an excellent, hardy, robust grower making a bushy, spreading, leafy shrub some 5ft × 5ft (1.5 × 1.5m). The flowers, in the usual clusters of the family, are semi-double and an attractive blend of crimson and mauve. A good repeat but not a great deal of scent.

**Pax** Pemberton, 1918. 'Trier' × 'Sunburst'. 6ft × 6ft (1.8 × 1.8m) and lax and arching, this carries the largest flowers of all the Hybrid Musks. They are semi-double and of a waxy white with a hint of yellow in the centre and large, golden stamens. A strong scent.

**Penelope** Pemberton, 1924. 'Ophelia' × an unnamed seedling or possibly 'William Allen Richardson' or 'Trier'. The flowers, which come at midsummer in small trusses and in much larger ones which practically obscure the leaves, are a lovely blend of cream and coppery-pink, with sometimes a hint of pale yellow. They are semi-double and rather loosely formed and some will be present at all times, though the autumn flush can be variable. Sometimes it can be tremendous, sometimes not so good, but almost always there will be at least one or two of the enormous new canes I referred to earlier bearing unbelievably large numbers of blooms. These are followed by quite attractive but not very showy greyish-pink hips. A very rugged grower to 6ft × 5ft (1.8 × 1.5m) at least, branching widely from low down and with good, semi-glossy leaves, dark green and with ruby-red edges when they first appear. AGM 1956. See Pl. 14.

**Pink Prosperity** Bentall, 1931. Dark leaves and dark red stems on a sturdy, rather upright, 5ft × 4ft (1.5 × 1.2m) bush. The large flower trusses have small, double, scented blooms of a clear, bright pink, fading paler but produced very freely. They are at their most perfect at the half-open stage. A sport from 'Prosperity' and not quite so vigorous. Strong fragrance.

**Prosperity** Pemberton, 1919. 'Marie-Jeanne' × 'Perle des Jardins'. Similar to 'Pink Prosperity' but probably reaching 7ft (2.1m) and with flowers a blend of cream and pink, fading white.

**Thisbe** Pemberton, 1918. A 'Daphne' sport? One that can be used for bedding, as it only reaches 4ft × 4ft (1.2 × 1.2m). The richly scented blooms are semi-double, opening into rosettes of buff-yellow and fading to cream. They have amber stamens. Lighter green leaves than most of the family.

**Vanity** Pemberton, 1920. 'Château de Clos Vougeot' × a seedling. The only Hybrid Musk with single flowers, and distinctive in other ways as well. It will easily reach 8–9ft (2.4–2.7m) and is even more prone than others of the group to send out enormous rigid branches at unexpected angles, crowned with immense corymbs of deep rose-pink flowers, a lighter colour in the autumn, and which have a sweet but not too strong perfume. As there are less leaves than there might be, three or four bushes can be planted together about a yard apart (if you have room for a group that will be at the very least 15ft (4.5m) across), when it will make a more compact and most spectacular display. Because it is so much taller it should not be put in the middle of a hedge of other Hybrid Musks. Maybe at the end. AM 1956, FCC 1958. See Pl. 14.

**Wilhelm** ('Skyrocket') Kordes, 1934. 'Robin Hood' × 'J.C. Thornton'. A robust and upright grower, reaching 7ft × 5ft (2.1 × 1.5m) or 10ft (3m) if grown on a pillar. Only slightly fragrant, it blooms very freely with trusses of 3in (7.5cm) semi-double, crimson flowers which are lighter in colour towards the centre and have golden stamens. There is some fade in strong sunlight, when the petals can take on a bluish tinge. Medium-sized red hips follow. Almost thornless.

**Will Scarlet** Introduced by Hilling, 1948. A 'Wilhelm' sport. Very similar to its parent except for the colour of its flowers, which are lighter and more nearly approaching scarlet, once again with the paling towards the centre. AM 1954.

## Chapter 13

# Polyanthas

Now I find myself in an embarrassing position, with an apology due to the nursery trade. Having taken them to task (I hope without rancour) for putting Polyantha roses in with the Chinas in their catalogues, I am now going to put roses which are not strictly Polyanthas into this chapter. Like the nurserymen I can only plead convenience, feeling, nevertheless, about as small as a garden gnome.

It could be argued, I suppose, that Polyanthas have no place in 'this book at all, as they are neither old nor modern shrub roses. My justification must be that they fit in very well with both of them, and their small stature helps to complete a picture otherwise mainly composed of fairly or very large bushes. In the same way, I will be discussing climbers and ramblers later on, which take us upwards rather than downwards, though a number of these, as distinct from the Polyanthas, are contemporaries of the old roses.

The Polyanthas, or Poly-poms as they are sometimes called, were the immediate forerunners of the modern Floribundas and differ from them mainly in their smaller stature and smaller flowers. They in their turn descended in a direct line from the white, cluster-flowered Japanese rambler R. *polyantha*, which subsequently had its name changed to R. *multiflora*. This was crossed by the French breeder Guillot (who also bred the first Hybrid Tea), almost certainly with a China rose. His first Polyantha variety, 'Ma Pâquerette', came in 1875.

At the time there was nothing like these new roses. Small and compact and later on in gay colours, they covered a range from white through pinks and reds to crimson, though yellows were rather rare. A more modern variety, 'Paul Crampel', actually beat 'Super Star' in the vermilion stakes, but as a class they did have some faults. Presumably because of their close link with a rambler they mildewed badly, and a second though less serious problem was their tendency to sport, which could make a shambles of a bedding scheme if only one colour was wanted.

If these two things are true, the question must once more be asked: why are they being recommended for planting in modern gardens? What have they got to offer that the low-growing families such as the China roses have not?

Apart from their appeal as part of rose history, which will be justification enough in some eyes for selecting at least a few, the answer is that I have picked out only some of the best survivors of the main line of Polyantha development. Others included here are dwarf sports of different ramblers, which also figure in the actual parentage of yet further varieties. They are a mixed bunch.

**Bloomfield Abundance**  Thomas, 1920. Although the parentage 'Sylvia' × 'Dorothy Page-Roberts' is given for this, there is a strong and growing school of thought that holds that it is a sport of 'Cécile Brunner'. I agree with this, because it is difficult to imagine two completely different sets of parents producing roses not only with almost identical flowers, but ones which are unlike those of any other rose. So let us say that it is a Tea-Polyantha as 'Cécile Brunner' is; that is, a Tea rose crossed with a Polyantha rambler. The tiny, thimble-sized, flesh-pink blooms certainly resemble the later Tea roses in the bud and they open into informal rosettes. In all of this they are identical to those of 'Cécile Brunner', but the calyces of the buds in this case have very long, feathery lobes, so that they seem to be wearing a plume. This is the easiest way to tell the two roses apart, but 'Bloomfield Abundance' also makes a much bigger bush, often topping 6ft (1.8m), quite open and airy, nearly thornless and with small, rather pointed leaves. It bears smallish sprays of flowers in early summer, and later is apt to send up enormously vigorous shoots many feet in length and with huge corymbs of bloom at the ends and further smaller sprays on numerous side shoots. Polyanthas are small and compact, I seem to remember saying, and here once again the alphabet compels us to start off with a giant, but Jack Harkness holds it to be a hybrid China and not a Polyantha at all, so perhaps this is why.

**Cameo**  de Ruiter, 1932. A really compact, bushy shrub going up to no more than 1ft 6in (45cm). The clusters of china-pink flowers come freely over a long period and there is a good repeat.

**Cécile Brunner** Pernet-Ducher, 1881. Polyantha ×'Madame de Tartas'. I have already said a good deal about this when describing 'Bloomfield Abundance' and the flowers have been fully described. It makes a bush about 3–4ft (1–1.2m) high, with open, not particularly robust-looking but quite hardy growth, which will take two or three years to reach full stature. It can be used for bedding where quiet charm is more important than fireworks, or a clump of two or three together on the corner of a patio can be very pleasing. Do not overdo the pruning, only removing dead or weak and diseased growth. With good cultivation it will reward you with a nonstop succession of blooms for the buttonhole.

**The Fairy** Introduced by Bentall, 1932. A dwarf sport of the rambler 'Lady Godiva'. The short, stiff canes, bright green to match the glossy leaves, come with the utmost profusion, bearing large trusses of soft pink, very double and globular blooms, which hold their shape and colour until the petals drop, unless there is prolonged rain when they may turn brown, but are unfortunately scentless. Ideal for a low hedge or for bordering a path or drive, it will reach 2ft 6in (76cm), spreading out quite widely. Blooming is more or less continuous, but a lookout must be kept for black spot. See Pl. 10.

**Little White Pet** Introduced by Henderson, 1879. A sport of the rambler 'Félicité et Perpétue', it keeps on producing flowers long after its parent has stopped, a phenomenon by no means uncommon with rambler sports. A 2ft × 2ft (60 × 60cm) bush, it is a rose that can add distinction to a rockery, or in small groupings be used at the front of a shrub border that is fully in the sun. I have also seen it making a most attractive standard. The 1½in (4cm), short-petalled and very double flowers are carried in both large and small clusters, creamy-white to blush, and opening flat. The small, dark green foliage is in pleasant contrast. Only a rumour of scent.

**Margo Koster** Koster, 1931. Sport of 'Dick Koster'. The cupped, salmon-pink flowers are borne on a bushy plant reaching 1ft 6in (45cm). At one time widely used as a pot plant, but a useful edging rose in the garden. Slight fragrance only.

**Marie Pavié** 1880. A little taller than the previous two, in that it will reach about 3ft (1m), healthy and robust. Sprays of small flowers varying in colour from blush to pale pink.

**Nathalie Nypels** Leenders, 1919. 'Orléans Rose' × ('Comtesse du Cayla' × R. *foetida bicolor*). A really charming little rose, useful for bedding on a small scale, for it only grows to about 2ft × 2ft (60 × 60cm), but it is bushy and well filled out with dark green leaves. From early summer onwards it will be covered with large clusters of 2½in (6cm) semi-double, cupped, rose-pink flowers which fade almost to white after a time but still look well. It is as good as most and better than many Floribundas of similar size. Good scent, but it can mildew. Some doubt about parentage.

**Paul Crampel** Kersbergen, 1930. A rather more orange vermilion than that of 'Super Star' but by no means dissimilar, this rose has fine trusses of double blooms, globular in shape. It will reach 2ft (60cm) in height, but beware of mildew on the light green, matt leaves. Only regular spraying will make this a worthwhile novelty, but since it is still not difficult to obtain its merits seem to outweigh this drawback in the eyes of many. Not, on balance, with me.

**Perle d'Or** Rambaud, 1884. Polyantha × 'Madame Falcot'? A Tea-Polyantha and not too unlike 'Cécile Brunner' in many ways. Generally a 4ft × 3ft (1.2 × 1m) bush, though on occasions I have seen it a great deal bigger – up to half as much again – so be prepared. It flowers freely and continuously, the small double blooms coming from yellow buds and opening cream, shading to orange-apricot in the centre.

**Yesterday** Harkness, 1973. ('Phyllis Bide' × 'Shepherd's Delight') × 'Ballerina'. Officially classified at the time of its introduction as a Floribunda-Polyantha, this is a small, airy shrub which could easily be mistaken for a China rose. Almost always in flower, the delicate sprays of small, semi-double blooms, which open flat, are a fairly deep lilac-pink, much lighter in the centre. Shiny, healthy leaves add their attractions to a bush which will not often top 3ft (1m), but which will branch out freely all round.

**Yvonne Rabier** Turbat, 1910. R. *wichuraiana* × a Polyantha. A fine, bushy grower to 3ft 6in (107cm) if pruned lightly (as it should be), and extremely free-flowering. Sprays of small, double, strongly scented white flowers in small clusters are carried over a long period.

*Chapter 14*

# Modern Shrub Roses

THESE are a really mixed bunch, and I can say with considerable relief that it is impossible to make any generalisations about them as a family. Too often in earlier chapters I have tried to do so and then the first rose in the variety descriptions is a maverick, but here I can say from the start that many kinds and families of roses are involved. They include what are essentially tall-growing Floribundas such as 'Fred Loads', 'Chinatown' and 'Dorothy Wheatcroft'; tall-growing Hybrid Teas such as 'Alexander' and 'Uncle Walter' and even 'Peace'; modern hybrids that resemble the old garden roses and often have one in their immediate parentage, as have 'Constance Spry' and 'Fritz Nobis'; hybrids closely related to species and in many ways resembling them, such as 'Golden Wings'; and finally many other roses of mixed parentage which have, possibly to their breeders' delight, and certainly to ours, turned out to be shrubs which would add distinction to any garden.

In addition to this there is a fairly large group, a great many of which came from the breeding programme of the late Wilhelm Kordes, which are often listed as pillar roses; that is, as short climbers and sometimes as strong-growing informal shrubs. They are equally good in either role and among them are 'Maigold' and 'Dortmund' from Germany, and from America, 'Joseph's Coat' and 'Aloha'. To look at, the latter might almost be a Bourbon.

As it is clearly impossible to make comments about use, cultivation, pruning and so on that will cover them all, any special points about a particular rose will be made under the individual variety description.

**Alexander** Harkness, 1972. 'Super Star' × ('Ann Elizabeth' × 'Allgold'). The colour of 'Super Star' caused a sensation when it first came out and made it a very popular favourite until suddenly its

108

health became suspect and mildew became a problem. Well, here are the striking vermilion tones again, though rather deeper, on flowers that are shapely at first but open somewhat informally. Several to a stem, they come with great freedom over a long period with only a brief pause between flushes. Upright in habit, it will reach 5ft (1.5m). The strong canes have dark, semi-glossy leaves which are generally very healthy. Good in rainy weather. RNRS C of M 1972.

**Aloha** Boerner, 1949. 'Mercedes Gallart' × 'The New Dawn'. Used as a climber this will reach about 10ft (3m), though it will take quite a long time about it. As, however, it is one of the comparatively few climbers that is *truly* remontant, it is worth waiting for, its one possible disadvantage being the very long and straight flowering stems, with a cluster of bloom at the end of each, which have to be tied in quite frequently. On the other hand they are fairly thornless, which makes them wonderful for cutting, and the flowers last well in the house. As a 5ft × 3ft (1.5 × 1m) shrub the long stems are no problem and it is equally good in this form, with, of course, the same first-rate glossy foliage, on which I have never seen disease of any sort. It sets off perfectly the large and very double, warm pink, strongly scented, rain-proof flowers, which have a hint of flame at the heart in their early stages. The half-open buds look unpromising, but do not be put off by this. Just wait. Little pruning is needed other than the occasional shortening of the side shoots in winter. See Pl. 11.

**Angelina** Cocker, 1975. ('Super Star' × 'Carina') × ('Cläre Grammerstorf' × 'Frühlingsmorgen'). A rose yet to make its name, but if there is any justice it must do exactly that. Excellent for a low hedge or for the front of the border, or indeed it could be used for bedding. It makes a strong-growing, rounded bush of about 3–4ft (1–1.2m) and as much across, ideal for a small garden. Healthy, matt, light green leaves and trusses of 3in (7.5cm), semi-double flowers of deep pink with a white eye and yellow stamens, opening cupped to flat. Fully remontant. RNRS C of M 1976. See Pl. 11.

**Berlin** Kordes, 1949. 'Eva' × 'Peace'. I do not know where the 'Peace' side of the family went to, for 'Berlin' has large trusses, intermittently produced, of 3½in (9cm), single, orange-scarlet flowers of great brilliance but with very little scent. An upright, 4ft × 3ft (1.2 × 1m) shrub with the habit of a large cluster flowered bush rose, large, dark leaves, and distinctive red thorns. I suppose that 'Peace' could have given it, in a negative sort of way, its lack of scent. RNRS TGC 1950.

**Bonn** Kordes, 1950. 'Hamburg' × 'Independence'. One to grow behind others as it tends to be leggy and will reach 6ft × 4ft (1.8 × 1.2m). The leaves are large, glossy, light green and leathery, and the 3in (7.5cm) flowers are a mixture of deep salmon and orange-scarlet, very showy until, as may happen, they fade to a not particularly attractive purplish tint. They are double but rather loosely formed. Little scent, although this rose is related to the Hybrid Musks. It needs dead-heading if a long flowering season is to be achieved, but will produce large, deep red hips in the autumn. C of M 1950, AM 1962.

**Butterfly Wings** Gobbee, 1976. 'Dainty Maid' × 'Peace'. Once again 'Peace' has helped to produce an offspring that has not the slightest resemblance to it, and this is one of the few roses in commerce that was raised by an amateur. It is an upright grower with stiff canes, to about 4ft (1.2m), reasonably bushy and making a sizeable plant. The flowers, in medium-sized clusters, are enchanting, about 3in (7.5cm) across, single to semi-double, and creamy-white with cerise-pink at the petal edges. Those who know the climber 'Handel' will get the picture, and the flowers are, of course, remontant. Good, mid-green leaves.

**Chinatown** ('Ville de Chine') Poulsen, 1963. 'Columbine' × 'Cläre Grammerstorf'. Long, strong canes and plenty of them make this an upright grower, well covered with exceptionally fine bright green and generally healthy leaves – though black spot is not unknown late in the season. It has been said of 'Chinatown' that it spends more of its energy in making leaves than flowers, but I cannot agree, though they are plentiful and help to make it a first-rate hedging rose. In my experience it bears its full quota of flower trusses, each with up to seven or eight very large, weather-proof, double, clear bright yellow blooms, sometimes with just a hint of pink about them. This is a rose that might well have had 'Peace' as an immediate parent, for they are not dissimilar, but here the

110

flowers are much more strongly coloured and very sweetly scented. Prune lightly as for a Floribunda, which, in fact, this is. FCC 1967, RNRS GM 1962.

**Clair Matin** Meilland, 1960. 'Fashion' × [('Independence' × 'Orange Triumph') × 'Phyllis Bide']. Large and small clusters of medium-sized, semi-double, light flesh-pink flowers in tremendous profusion which open to show golden stamens and have a sweet scent. The light green foliage on the spreading, 5ft × 7ft (1.5 × 2.1m) bush is sometimes crimson-tinted and is generally free from disease. There are two distinct flowering periods.

**Constance Spry** Austin, 1961. 'Belle Isis' × 'Dainty Maid'. This will make a large and well-rounded bush with strong, long canes, probably about 7ft × 7ft (2.1 × 2.1m), the leaves coppery when young, changing to dark green. Some of the more lax branches may need support from surrounding shrubs, or the rose can be grown on a tripod, and all will bear along almost their entire length double flowers that can be as much as 6in (15cm) across. They come in heads of several together, not as fragrant as one would hope, but cupped in shape and of a clear rose-pink. Certainly this is one of the best of the modern shrubs that follow the old style, and like the old ones it flowers only at midsummer, though over a long period. AM 1965.

**Dorothy Wheatcroft** Tantau, 1960. As with so many of this leading German breeder's roses, no parentage is given. A very tall-growing, upright shrub which needs to be placed behind something else if it is to look its best. It will reach 5ft (1.5m) or so, each of the long, strong canes crowned by huge clusters of semi-double, 3in (7.5cm) flowers, officially described as orient red or, less technically, orange-scarlet with deeper shadings. They make an eye-catching show, though there can be a slightly purplish tinge to them in the last stages. The petals have scalloped edges and stand up well to rain, which is a good thing as the blooms are tightly packed in the truss. Only a slight scent, but healthy, glossy, medium-green leaves. A good repeat. AM 1960, RNRS GM 1961.

**Dortmund** Kordes, 1955. Seedling × R. *kordesii*. This may be found in catalogues either as a shrub or as a pillar rose, and it is equally good in each role. As the former it will be lax but freely branching, with dark, glossy, rather pointed leaves and something like 5ft × 8ft (1.5 × 2.4m). As a climber it will go up to 8ft (2.4m), and in both forms bears trusses of very large (4in or 10cm), single, crimson-red flowers with a most distinctive white eye and buff-yellow stamens. Dead-heading is necessary for it to be fully remontant.

**Elmshorn** Kordes, 1951. 'Hamburg' × 'Verdun'. 5–6ft (1.5–1.8m) tall and about the same across, this makes a well-branched bush which needs a distinct rest between the first flush of bloom and the second. The 1½in (4cm) flowers are fully double, cup-shaped, and come in large trusses. They are of a brilliant deep carmine-pink, which can make them difficult to place in relation to other roses. Certainly they should be kept away from anything approaching scarlet. Not much scent; small, dark, glossy leaves. Can be grown on a pillar.

**Erfurt** Kordes, 1939. 'Eva' × 'Reveil Dijonnais'. With 'Eva' as one parent this could legitimately appear among the Hybrid Musks and it is one of the loveliest of the Kordes group of roses. Clear rose-pink flowers freely produced in clusters, the white centres often tinted pale primrose and each having a very prominent boss of deep golden stamens. The bush is spreading and arching, building up to about 5ft × 6ft (1.5 × 1.8m), the leaves having an attractive coppery tint when young. They are healthy, with the bush in flower for most of the summer. Scented. See Pl. 11.

**Eye Paint** McGredy, 1976. ('Little Darling' × 'Goldilocks') × ['Evelyn Fison' × ('Coryana' × 'Tantau's Triumph')]. A shrubby grower for the small garden, with masses of mid-green, semi-glossy leaves and large trusses of smallish single flowers of the brightest scarlet with a white eye. The petal reverse is paler. The stamens are orange. No scent, but both continuity and weather resistance are good. Reaching about 4ft (1.2m), it makes an excellent low hedge, although black spot can be a problem. A striking and unusual rose, however. RNRS TGC 1973. See Pl. 12.

**First Choice** Morse, 1958. 'Masquerade' × 'Sultane'. Essentially an extra-vigorous Floribunda, reaching 4–5ft (1.2–1.5m) after a year or two if not too heavily pruned. It bears, when they are newly opened, some of the most spectacular flowers of any rose. They are single but enormous, some 4½in (11cm) across, with butterfly-like petals in the brightest orange-scarlet, shading to yellow in the centre and with a pale, yellowish-pink – or pinkish-yellow – reverse. As the petals are waved, this second colour can be clearly seen on the truss and forms a most striking contrast to the fiery red. Unfortunately they have inherited from 'Masquerade' the habit of changing to a rather ugly dark pinkish-red as they age, so dead-heading should be carried out promptly. Good rain resistance, but not much scent. The bush branches freely and many new, plum-red canes come from the base each year. The leaves are dark green and generally healthy. RNRS C of M 1958. See Pl. 11.

**Fountain** Tantau, 1971. Another Tantau mystery rose, a very tall and upright one of enormous vigour, the strong green canes going up to about 6ft (1.8m), but not spreading out much beyond 3ft 6in (107cm). Most, though not all, of the double, scented flowers come fairly high up, and are large, well-shaped at first but opening informally with waved petals. They are a rich, velvety deep scarlet and are generally carried in clusters of from four to six. Large and very handsome matt, dark green leaves, covering the plant well. RNRS GM 1971.

**Frank Naylor** Harkness, 1978. [('Orange Sensation' × 'Allgold') × ('Little Lady' × 'Little Charm')] × [('Blue Moon' × 'Magenta') × ('Cläre Grammerstorf' × 'Frühlingsmorgen')]. An incredibly mixed bag of parents has produced a most distinctive, not to say distinguished rose. It makes a bushy, shrubby plant up to about 4ft (1.2m) with plentiful, very dark, purplish-green leaves and carrying sprays of small, single flowers in crimson-maroon and with golden centres. It makes a striking and unusual hedge, and a scented one too. Good in the rain. Early and remontant. RNRS TGC.

**Fred Loads** Holmes, 1968. 'Dorothy Wheatcroft' × 'Orange Sensation'. Another one raised by an amateur and the vigour of 'Dorothy Wheatcroft' can only in part account for the enormous size to which it will grow. Certainly it did not come from 'Orange Sensation', noted for its short stature, because 'Fred Loads' will send up its strong, rigid canes to something like 7ft (2.1m), but they are quite freely branching so that there is a reasonable spread, and plenty of light green, semi-glossy leaves that do not seem much troubled by disease. The flowers come in trusses that can exceed 18in (45cm) in width, each one about 4in (10cm) in diameter, single, and of the most lovely light vermilion-orange, paling a little towards the centre and sweetly scented. Can be used as a specimen shrub (it is remontant), for hedges, or if planted in groups of three or four it will be sensational. AM 1967, RNRS GM 1967.

**Fritz Nobis** Kordes, 1940. 'Joanna Hill' × 'Magnifica'. The second parent here was a self-seedling of the little-known Penzance Brier 'Lucy Ashton', so that it is really an R. *rubiginosa* hybrid and in consequence is once-flowering only, though it puts on a display that lasts for weeks. The semi-double blooms are shapely at first but open with attractively waved petals of the softest salmon-pink blending into blush-pink. The bush is rounded and full, some 6ft × 6ft (1.8 × 1.8m), and has glossy, leathery leaves and a fair sprinkling of dark red, rounded but not very showy hips in the autumn. Makes a wonderful specimen shrub. A bridal bouquet rose. AM 1959. See Pl. 12.

**Frühlingsanfang** see p.38.

**Frühlingsduft** see p.38.

**Frühlingsgold** see p.38.

**Frühlingsmorgen** see p.38.

**Goldbusch** Kordes, 1954. A 5ft × 6ft (1.5 × 1.8m) rose, equally good as a free-standing shrub, when it will spread out wide, or on a pillar, and with glossy, light green leaves. Midsummer-flowering and remontant, it has attractive, salmon-flushed buds, opening to semi-double blooms in a mixture of peach-pink and pale yellow and with golden stamens. Scented. AM 1965.

**Golden Chersonese** Allen, 1969. R. *ecae* × 'Canary Bird'. A modern cross between two wild roses, which it resembles in many ways, though the bright yellow flowers are smaller and of a more intense

114

yellow than 'Canary Bird', but are bigger than those of R. *ecae*. Like both of them it is spring-flowering only, starting very early, and forms a bushy, twiggy, upright but arching 6ft × 7ft (1.8 × 2.1m) shrub with small but plentiful dainty leaves. Some scent. AM 1966, RNRS C of M 1970.

**Golden Moss** Dot, 1932. 'Frau Karl Druschki' × ('Souvenir de Claudius Pernet' × 'Blanche Moreau'). Although nothing like as old as most Moss roses, this does follow the general pattern of growth, with 6ft (1.8m) lax canes and the dark green leaves of the Damask Moss which is on one side of the family. The double blooms are, however, canary-yellow, though this fades rather rapidly to a creamy-yellow except in the heart of the flower. A Moss in this colour takes some getting used to and, illogically, does not seem quite right. It is remontant, though the first, midsummer blooming is by far the best.

**Golden Wings** Shepherd, 1956. 'Soeur Thérèse' × (R. *spinosisima altaica* × 'Ormiston Roy'). A gem. The large single flowers come in medium-sized clusters on a 5–6ft (1.5–1.8m) fairly upright bush which will in time branch out to about the same distance. They are pale yellow, deepening towards the centre, and have amber stamens, not unlike those of the climber 'Mermaid'. Two tremendous flushes and always blooms in between, but the removal of the first hips does help. They are not, in any case, a decorative feature. The matt, light green leaves are seemingly disease-proof and are notably long and pointed. Takes easily from cuttings. AM 1965. See Pl. 12.

**Gruss an Aachen** Geduldig, 1909. Held by some people to be the first Floribunda, but one parent was the Hybrid Perpetual 'Frau Karl Druschki' and the other the Hybrid Tea 'Franz Deegen'. Let us say that, retrospectively, it turned out to be a rose in the Floribunda mould, for it is a small one, not more than 2ft 6in (76cm) tall and spreading out to about the same. It bears a mass of large, scented, creamy flesh-pink, very double blooms which open flat, and is remontant. The rich green leaves may need watching for mildew. Included here as an ideal rose for the front of the shrub border and which looks quite at home with the old garden varieties.

**Heidelberg** Kordes, 1959. Tough and very hardy, this makes a 5–6ft × 4ft (1.5–1.8 × 1.2m) fairly upright plant with a moderate lateral spread and with plenty of glossy, bronze-tinted, dark green, healthy leaves. The large flowers come in clusters, between semi-double and double, and are of an intense crimson-scarlet, fading slightly and with little scent. It will grow anywhere and so is useful for a difficult spot in the garden, though not, of course, in heavy shade. A good autumn display. On a pillar it will go up to 7ft (2.1m).

**Hunter** Mattock, 1961. R. *rugosa rubra* × 'Independence'. Although a Rugosa hybrid, the leaves are those of a Hybrid Tea. A profuse and remontant bloomer, with bright crimson double flowers, it will make a good informal hedge.

**Iceberg** ('Schneewittchen', 'Fée des Neiges') Kordes, 1958. 'Robin Hood' × 'Virgo'. One of the best Floribundas ever raised, regardless of colour, this can grow, if not severely pruned, into a fairly tall shrub about 5ft (1.5m) high and 3ft (1m) across. The 3in (7.5cm) blooms are carried in both large and small sprays all over the bush at all levels on the slender canes, and not just at the top as with so many of the type. Sometimes tinted pink in the bud, they open, camellia-like, to pure white and are delicately scented. Two magnificent flushes of bloom and always some flowers in between. They stand up well to rain, though there can be some pink spotting if it is prolonged. Reports indicate that it is possibly becoming increasingly prone to mildew and black spot, but I have not found this to be so myself. The light green, plentiful foliage has always been healthy enough with me. RNRS GM 1958.

**Joseph's Coat** Armstrong and Swim, 1964. 'Buccaneer' × 'Circus'. This can be used as a short climber, though its long, strong canes can be difficult to train. As a shrub it will reach 6ft (1.8m), branching and arching out to 8ft (2.4m) or more in a rather haphazard way, with healthy, abundant, glossy, mid-green leaves. The flowers are prolific at midsummer with a less spectacular autumn flush and a few in between. Spectacular is the right word to use, too, for 'Joseph's Coat' bears large sprays of 3in (7.5cm) semi-double blooms in a mixture of gold, orange and cherry-red, shaded and veined a deeper orange. Very little scent, but makes a fine informal hedges. RNRS TGC 1963, AM 1966. See Pl. 11.

**Kathleen Ferrier** Buisman, 1952. 'Gartenstolz' × 'Shot Silk'. A rose few seem to have heard of and even fewer grow, and it is very difficult to understand why. Imagine the beautiful 'Fred Loads' – always assuming you know it, of course – but with soft salmon-pink flowers and not such demanding vigour, together with a rather more spreading habit, and you have 'Kathleen Ferrier'. It will probably reach 5–6ft (1.5–1.8m), with its huge trusses of bloom in remarkable profusion and fully remontant. The dark, glossy leaves seem generally healthy. AM 1963.

**La France** Guillot, 1867. Possibly 'Madame Victor Verdier' × 'Madame Bravy' or 'Madame Falcot'. Of course this should not be here at all, and is only included because it was the first of the Hybrid Teas. Admittedly one or two others have been or will be described, but only because they grow to such a size that they can truly be called shrub roses. 'La France', on the other hand, seems to have lost some of its vigour over the years; I have seen it depicted in old rose books as reaching 4–5ft (1.2–1.5m). The strain available nowadays, however, makes a moderately vigorous upright bush, not often exceeding 3ft × 2ft (1m × 60cm), but it is such a landmark as a variety that to my mind a place has to be found for it in any book dealing mainly with the old roses. Its date of introduction is earlier than many of the Hybrid Perpetuals and in fact it might be the runt of the litter of that group, having been classed as such at one time. It carries two main flushes of large, fairly globular blooms in silvery-pink with a darker reverse, a little loosely petalled by modern standards, but they hold their shape over a respectable period and are more resistant to rain than some reports suggest. Plentiful, shiny, mid-green leaves, not entirely proof against mildew in the second half of the season.

**Lavender Lassie** Kordes, 1960. Parents unknown. Enormous heads of very double, short-petalled, 3in (7.5cm) blooms of the pompon type, and although the long, strong canes are unlikely to bend very much, the weight of the trusses of bloom, especially after rain, will make them lean outwards so that the support of a stake is advised. With this, it can be kept quite compact and will reach 4–5ft (1.2–1.5m). Despite its name, I have never been able to detect any lavender colouring in the blooms, which I would describe as a pure, soft rose-pink, fading paler. And once again, though scent is claimed, it largely eludes me. Good, very healthy and very glossy light green foliage. For a rose so crammed with petals it stands rain well. See Pl. 12.

**Leverkusen** Kordes, 1954. R. *kordesii* ×'Golden Glow'. A climber or shrub, as you wish. Large sprays of rosette-type, double, scented flowers in lemon-yellow on a robust, gracefully arching bush of about 5ft × 4ft (1.5 × 1.2m) or going up to 10ft (3m) on a pillar. Deep green, glossy leaves, somewhat on the small side, blend well with the flowers which put on a fine display at mid-summer but are less prolific later on. It will make a good hedge.

**Maigold** Kordes, 1953. 'Poulsen's Pink' × 'Frühlingstag'. A really big, 7ft × 8ft (2.1 × 2.4m) rambling and very thorny shrub, or else a fine 15ft (4.5m) climber for a wall, fence or pergola. It flowers in late spring with a grand display over several weeks and if the spent flowers are removed there can be some further, intermittent bloom. The 3in (7.5cm) flowers are semi-double, loosely cupped in shape and bronze-yellow, shading to flesh-pink at the edges of the petals and with crimson, gold-tipped stamens. A good fragrance and medium-green, glossy leaves.

**Marguerite Hilling** see p.33.

**Marjorie Fair** Harkness, 1977. 'Ballerina' × 'Baby Faurax'. In almost every way an exact counterpart of 'Ballerina', but with flowers in a dark ruby red with a white eye.

**Nevada** see p.33.

**Nymphenburg** Kordes, 1954. 'Sangerhausen' × 'Sunmist'. A first-rate, arching, informal shrub reaching 6ft × 6ft (1.8 × 1.8m), or going up to 18ft (5.5m) on a wall if it is used as a climber. Great clusters of large and very double blooms of salmon-pink with golden tints and a yellow base to the petals. Handsome, large, dark, glossy leaves and a sweet scent.

**Peace** ('Gioia', 'Gloria Dei', 'Madame A. Meilland') Meilland, 1945. [('George Dickson' × 'Souvenir de Claudius Pernet') × ('Joanna Hill' × 'Charles P. Kilham')] × 'Margaret McGredy'.

Probably the most famous and certainly the most popular Hybrid Tea ever raised, and hardly needing a detailed description. In most cases used as a bedding rose, if lightly pruned ('Peace' should never be pruned hard anyway) it will make a 4–6ft (1.2–1.8m) specimen planting or a hedge shrub with wonderful, healthy, glossy green leaves as a background to its unsurpassed, huge, pale yellow flowers. Blind shoots – those with no flower buds – can appear in early summer on this rose, but if these are cut back to a good strong side bud new flowering shoots should quickly follow. Do not expect 'Peace' to show colour very early. It is a notoriously late starter into bloom.

**Poulsen's Park Rose** Poulsen, 1953. 'Great Western' × 'Karen Poulsen'. On the Continent large shrub roses are far more popular in parks than they are elsewhere and are used extensively in vast bedding schemes. Hence the name of this one from Denmark, a robust, 5ft × 5ft (1.5 × 1.5m) shrub, with both large and small heads of light pink, semi-double, fragrant blooms. Good foliage borne on deep red canes. A spectacular first show at midsummer, a rest period, and then off it goes again, but it is not too happy in the rain.

**Queen Elizabeth** Lammerts, 1954. 'Charlotte Armstrong' × 'Floradora'. Like 'Peace' a rose that is seen everywhere, but too often in the wrong position in the garden, for it can be awkward to place. The reason for this is that it can grow enormously tall (8–9ft or 2.4–2.7m) and, if not properly pruned, have most of its lovely, slightly scented, cupped, silvery-pink flowers right at the top. An aching neck from looking up at them is the result, but there is something that can be done about this. Cutting back a fair proportion of the main canes each year by as much as half, and the others by one third, will help it to bush out and bear flowers lower down. It will still be tall and upright as that is its nature, but if treated in this way it will be more manageable and will make a wonderful hedge which will not take up a lot of space. Or, of course, it can be planted at the back of a border. The flowers come on long, thornless stems, singly and in medium-sized clusters, and 'Queen Elizabeth' is first-rate as a cutting rose for the house. Tolerant of rain and is generally one of the healthiest. Fine, dark green leaves. RNRS GM 1955.

**Radway Sunrise** Waterhouse Nurseries, 1962. A 'Masquerade' seedling. A strong-growing, well-branched and reasonably erect and not too large bush, reaching about 5ft × 4ft (1.5 × 1.2m). Remontant, the blooms are single, borne in clusters and in blends of flame and pink with buff-yellow centres, giving a gay and lively effect. Healthy, glossy, mid-green leaves. Especially good in the autumn.

**Raubritter** Kordes, 1936. R. × *macrantha* × 'Solarium'. The same spreading habit as the first of the two parents, so that it is unlikely to exceed 3ft (1m) in height, but its trailing branches will reach out to twice that at least. An ideal rose, therefore, for draping over walls or running down banks and, to a certain extent, for ground-cover. It can also be used at the front of a wide border and will, if given the chance, scramble into other shrubs. The dark leaves (not proof against mildew) form a fine background to the clustered blooms which are reminiscent in their globular form (which they hold throughout) of the Bourbon rose 'La Reine Victoria', though smaller. Clear pink, they come in great profusion at midsummer, but there is no repeat. Only slight fragrance.

**Sally Holmes** Holmes, 1978. 'Ivory Fashion' × 'Ballerina'. One of the very best of the newer shrub roses and yet to gain the reputation it undoubtedly deserves. Raised by the amateur also responsible for 'Fred Loads', it is every bit as good in its own way but is of more suitable proportions for a small garden because it will keep to a bushy 4–5ft (1.2–1.5m), with a fine coverage of always immaculate semi-glossy, mid-green leaves. It is remontant and the large trusses of single, 3½in (9cm) flowers are carried in great profusion, ivory-white, sometimes with a pink flush, especially at the petal edges. It will make an excellent hedge of medium height.

**Scarlet Fire** ('Scharlachglut') Kordes, 1952. 'Poinsettia' × 'Alika' (a Gallica hybrid). Very long, trailing branches make this an informal, free-ranging shrub to about 7ft × 7ft (2.1 × 2.1m) which can also be used as a pillar rose or grown against a fence. Once-flowering and only in the latter part of midsummer, the blooms, which come in clusters, are large, single and of the most breathtaking flaming scarlet, set off by golden stamens in the centre and followed by pear-shaped red hips. Someone once said 'if you've got it, flaunt it' and 'Scarlet Fire' does just this. The leaves are a matt mid-green and neither these, the flowers nor the habit of growth would indicate that this is, in fact, a Gallica hybrid. AM 1960.

**Scintillation** Austin, 1968. R. × *macrantha* × 'Vanity'. A 4ft (1.2m) lax and sprawling grower unless trained on a pillar or tripod. If left to itself it will scramble over hedges or old tree stumps, the long canes reaching out 6ft (1.8m) or more. Clusters of fragrant, semi-double blush-pink flowers.

**Sparrieshoop** Kordes, 1953. ('Baby Château' × 'Else Poulsen') × 'Magnifica'. A profuse but intermittent bloomer throughout the summer and autumn, this makes an upright 6ft × 4ft (1.8 × 1.2m) and rather open bush, with clusters of 4in (10cm) single, salmon-pink flowers carried on purplish-brown wood. The leaves, too, have a purple tint. The scented blooms, lovely at first, do not improve with time and should be removed regularly if they are not to spoil the effect of those waiting to replace them.

**Uncle Walter** McGredy, 1963. 'Detroiter' × 'Heidelberg'. This is a rose best placed at the back of a border or certainly with something low-growing in front of it, as it can be somewhat ungainly. It is, in fact, a very tall Hybrid Tea with the shapely blooms one would expect from that group. They come with great freedom at the end of long, strong canes, deep crimson-scarlet with a velvety sheen which does not, as happens with many roses of this colour, blue with age, but the scent is not marked. Handsome leaves, copper-tinted when young.

*Chapter 15*

# Ramblers

THESE are much more closely related to once-flowering species
than the climbers and are practically all nonremontant. By far the
biggest group have large heads of small flowers carried on the side
shoots of long, pliable canes, which can grow to incredible lengths
in the course of a year. New ones are constantly coming up from
the base of the plant.

A great many of the ramblers we grow are descended from the
comparatively late-flowering R. *wichuraiana* and so do not come
into bloom until well after the majority of climbers. Another,
smaller group (to which the well-known 'Albertine' and 'Albéric
Barbier' belong) derive from a rose closely related to R. *wichuraiana*
called R. *luciae*, have larger flowers in smaller clusters, bloom
much earlier and produce each year vigorous and rather stiffer
canes, not only from the base but also from some way up a number
of the old ones. Some other ramblers are wild roses in their own
right and yet others belong to the Ayrshire family which is
descended from R. *arvensis*, the Field Rose. Then there are those
that take their line from R. *sempervirens* or from R. *multiflora*. They
are a mixed bag.

Largely because they are nonremontant, ramblers are not grown
nowadays to anything like the extent they were when they first
burst on the scene in the early nineteenth century and continued in
popularity for something like one hundred years after that. At one
time they were a feature of almost every garden, putting on a
display which, for sheer quantity of bloom, few other roses of any
sort could match. They covered arches, pergolas, unsightly sheds
and old tree stumps and were used to form bowers which, as
Dickens put it, make 'those sweet retreats which humane men
erect for the accommodation of spiders'.

Well if tastes have changed, the ramblers have not. They are as good as ever for the purposes mentioned above and in addition make fine weeping standards. The one place it is best to keep them away from is a wall, for there air circulation will be poor and this will encourage mildew, to which some ramblers are particularly prone. They have, however, one use for which they are the roses *par excellence* and that is for growing up trees, where they can hook themselves from branch to branch to their hearts' content. There are several varieties, difficult to tell apart and practically inter-changeable, which have enormous heads of tiny white flowers and will scramble to an altitude of 30ft (9m) or more if a tree is big and strong enough to stand their weight and the added wind resistance they will create. The cascades of bloom that will hang down from the branches are one of the most lovely sights in the world and their fragrance will waft freely in the air.

**Albéric Barbier** Barbier, 1900. R. *luciae* × 'Shirley Hibberd'. A rampant rambler to 15ft (4.6m) or so for fences, trellis or pergolas, or for sprawling over dead tree stumps, and one of the healthiest there is. The foliage is extremely good, dark green with a bronze tint, glossy, and it stays on the plant well into the winter. The small yellow buds open to double, creamy-white flowers with a high, pointed centre at first, becoming more informal in shape later. Fading almost to white with age, they are fragrant and are produced in small clusters in tremendous profusion very early the summer. There may be a few later, but do not count on it. As they come on the side shoots of the previous year's growth, prune as for a climber rather than a rambler.

**Albertine** Barbier, 1921. R. *luciae* × 'Mrs Arthur Robert Waddell'. Probably even more vigorous than 'Albéric Barbier' and, in fact, difficult to curb in its exuberance. It can be grown in a number of ways, on a fence, pergola or pillar, but it is often sold as a weeping standard, in which form it can look very beautiful but, because of the stiffness of its canes, can be difficult to train. As an alternative it makes a very effective sprawling bush which in early summer will become a huge mound of blossom, sending out waves of scent into the air around. The flowers are large for a rambler, copper-pink in the bud and a soft pink with a high centre when opened, fading a little in hot sunshine. The odd shower will do little harm, but prolonged heavy rain can leave the petals a rather soggy mess, after which they will turn brown and not fall cleanly. The leaves are coppery to dark green, shiny, but unfortunately not proof against mildew, even if this does not usually become a problem until after the flowers are over. New canes, which come very freely, are a striking dark red. 'Albertine' will probably need fairly drastic pruning to keep it under control, but it is not one of the ramblers that needs cutting back to the base each year. Long side shoots will sprout from the main canes quite high up as well as low down, and it is these which should be shortened by at least two thirds and the old canes removed only from the point immediately above that from which the new ones have grown. This can be done once flowering is over. See Pl. 15.

**Bobbie James** Introduced by Graham Thomas at the Sunningdale Nurseries in 1960. Of unknown origin, but Mr Thomas considers it a Multiflora. Not a choice for a small garden, except possibly one that already has a tree so big that it ought to be somewhere else, for it will climb to 25ft (7.6m), branching out freely as it does so. Large clusters of semi-double, creamy-yellow flowers with yellow stamens come at midsummer only and will scent the air for yards around. Narrow, pointed, glossy leaves.

***R. brunonii* 'La Mortola'.** Probably a form of Brown's Musk rose from the Far East. Named after the famous Italian garden from which this particular strain came, it was only introduced in 1954. As this rose will go to 25ft (7.6m) or more it is difficult to suggest any form of shelter it could be given, except possibly the wall of an enormous house, but it does need something of the sort because it is not completely hardy except in a warm climate. It is a very fast grower with large trusses of creamy-white, 1in (2.5cm) flowers with golden stamens, which have the true Musk fragrance, and long, very pointed, grey-green, drooping leaves. Unusually for this type of rose, the blooms do not like rain.

**Emily Gray** Williams, 1918. 'Jersey Beauty' × 'Comtesse du Cayla'. I see that the bible of the rose world, *Modern Roses 8*, classes this as a large flowered climber, but as the first parent is a *wichuraiana* rambler and the second a China rose, I am venturing to differ. Certainly it has medium-sized to large, double, buff-yellow flowers in trusses, opening from yellow buds, and the dark green, glossy, healthy leaves are also on the big side for a rambler, but it is summer-flowering only. It will reach 15ft (4.5m) and is said by some to be not very hardy and also subject to die-back. From my own experience with it, this is not so. RNRS GM 1916.

**Félicité et Perpétue** Jacques, 1827. An R. *sempervirens* sport? A tough, hardy rambler and an exceptionally healthy one which will keep its dark green, glossy leaves for at least nine months of the year. The flowers come just after midsummer in clusters of varying size, blush-white, fading to white, and with hundreds of small petals that reflex into the most perfectly formed and regular pompons. Occasionally there can be quite a strong pink marking on some of the outer petals, but there is little, if any, scent. Freedom of flowering does, however, go a long way to make up for this. Probably reaching 12–15ft (3.7–4.5m) with long, slim branches that are easy to train, it is wonderful for a pillar or arch, but I also grow it as a low, sprawling bush, wandering over a dead stump that should have been dug out years ago. Considering how double they are, the blooms stand rain remarkably well. See Pl. 15.

**R. *filipes* 'Kiftsgate'** Introduced by Murrell, 1954. A sport of R. *filipes* and named after the Gloucestershire garden from which it came. The parent is from western China, allied to R. *moschata*. Plant and then get out of the way of the floral explosion, for it will spread wide in all directions, scrambling through and eventually overwhelming any but the very strongest form of support. 20–30ft (6–9m) is nothing to it, and it is a great climber into trees and other shrubs if you do not mind losing sight of them after a time. In the latter part of midsummer it will be smothered in vast heads of tiny creamy-white flowers, yellow-stamened and with an all-pervading fragrance.

**Francis E. Lester** Lester Rose Gardens, 1946. 'Kathleen' × un-named variety. This should not really be in this section, since it is actually a climbing Hybrid Musk, but in flower form and habit (except that it is remontant) it does more or less fit in with the ramblers. It originated in America, and following the rambler pattern it produces large clusters of small, very fragrant single blooms, which resemble apple blossom in their combination of pink and white. It will probably not go over 12ft (3.7m) as a rambler/climber, but as it branches freely it will also make a fine 7ft × 6ft (2.1 × 1.8m) bush with the help of a little support. Bright green, glossy leaves with, when young, the ruby-red edges one finds on such Hybrid Musks as 'Penelope', though the leaves themselves are longer and narrower than is typical of the type. Small, orange-red hips. A good tree-climber which is not too rampant.

**François Juranville** Barbier, 1906. R. *wichuraiana* × 'Madame Laurette Messimy'. From the same raiser as those flag-carriers for the ramblers, 'Albertine' and 'Albéric Barbier', but though every bit as good it has never for some reason achieved the same stardom. The flowers are fully double, opening flat, in a rich rose-pink with just a hint of golden-yellow at the centre and slightly quilled petals. On a pergola or open-work fence it will cover something like 25ft (7.6m) and there are fine, glossy leaves – bronze-tinted when young – and a spicy scent. Basically mid-summer flowering, there may also be a few late blooms.

**The Garland** Wells, 1835. R. *moschata* × R. *multiflora*. Considering its parentage, by no means a rampant grower as it will keep to about 15ft (4.5m). Sweetly scented with large clusters of semi-double, blush-pink blooms which fade fairly rapidly to white and are followed by small red hips. This was a favourite with Gertrude Jekyll, who was a great one for ramblers and knew all their qualities and failings. Her advice on this one was sadistic. Get up at 4 a.m. to admire the newly opened buds.

**Goldfinch** Paul, 1907. 'Hélène' × an unknown rose. A 10ft (3m) rose for pillars or for making an informal 6–7ft (1.8–2.1m) shrub which will weave its way through anything else planted near it. The clusters of strongly scented semi-double flowers are yellow, fading to cream, and come at midsummer with no repeat. Not one of the most prolific makers of new growth each year, but it will keep bushy if it is left unpruned.

*R. longicuspis* From western China and in cultivation since 1915. In its general characteristics this resembles R. *filipes* 'Kiftsgate' in many ways, but is better for cold districts and ones with difficult soils – even those with some chalk in them. And it is not

126

as overwhelming in size, though it is still a strong grower to about 20ft (6m). Well-displayed against the very glossy leaves, the flowers do not appear until after midsummer, but then what a show! Tiny, single and white, and coming in huge scented clusters, they are followed by minute red hips. Up a tree or on a pergola are positions to consider for it, and I have seen it used on the wall of a large house with great effect.

**Paul's Himalayan Musk Rambler** Introduced by George Paul, 1916. Definitely one for a big garden, for it will go up a tree to 40ft (12m). And think what that really means, for it would have to be a tree of 50–60ft (15–18m) if you allow for the usual slender top branches which would not bear the rose's weight; and that is a very big tree indeed. If the rose is used in this way, great swags of small, scented, blush-pink double flowers will hang down from late midsummer on. Or if used in a wild garden it could be allowed to form a vast, impenetrable mound of canes, which would be covered in blossom for several glorious weeks.

**Rambling Rector** A name with a real Victorian flavour to it, and it seems that the Rector rambled so far and so widely that he had not the slightest idea at the end of it where he had come from or when, though there is a suspicion that he must have encountered a Multiflora rambler on the way. It is another rose that bears masses of small (1½in or 3.5cm) white flowers, semi-double and fragrant, and as it will reach about 20ft (6m) and branches freely it is ideal for pergolas, or for screening tumble-down sheds or old tree stumps. It flowers at late midsummer. See Pl. 15.

**Ramona** ('Red Cherokee') A sport of R. × *anemonoides*, which is itself a hybrid of R. *laevigata* from China. Introduced in 1913, and there really is something Far Eastern about the large, single blooms that are a particularly pleasing blend of crimson lake and pale pink, with a pinkish-grey reverse to the petals. They look not unlike the flowers of a clematis, are scented and appear early, but only if you have a sheltered spot for it. Worth building a sunny wall especially for it.

**Seagull** Pritchard, 1907. A strongly perfumed, early summer flowering and not too vigorous rambler of the *rosa multiflora* type, and probably descended from it. Reaching about 12ft (3.7m), it is ideal for a pergola or for climbing into a small tree. Large trusses of single to semi-double white flowers with prominent golden stamens. Larger than most ramblers of this type. See Pl. 15.

**Seven Sisters** (R. *multiflora platyphylla*) Introduced in 1817, from China. This rose gets its intriguing name from the fact that the large clusters of semi-double flowers often have seven different tints at the same time, ranging from mauve, through pink to almost pure white, though how anyone could separate them out to count them I have never been able to discover. The blooms are much larger than those of R. *multiflora* itself. Strong-growing to 30ft (9m) and keeps in bloom over a long period.

**Silver Moon** Van Fleet, 1910. (R. *wichuraiana* × 'Devoniensis') × R. *laevigata*. A spectacularly lovely and very vigorous rambler, with fine, glossy, dark green leaves. The long, pointed, pale yellow buds open to 4½in (11.5cm) semi-double, creamy-white flowers with russet-gold stamens which appear in clusters on long-stemmed shoots. 40ft (12m) and not very much scent.

**Veilchenblau** Schmidt, 1909. 'Crimson Rambler' × anybody's guess. At certain stages probably the nearest to true blue of any rose, which is, when one comes to think of the roses that bear the word blue in their popular names, not really much of a claim. Typical rambler heads of small, semi-double flowers, opening purplish-blue to reveal a lilac-white eye and with occasional white streaks on the petals. Sweetly scented and with bright green, glossy canes and leaves. Mildew is a rarity on this one, and it will even do well on a north wall. 10–15ft (3–4.5m).

**Wedding Day** Stern, 1950. R. *sinowilsonii* ×? A comparatively modern rambler, but in the old style. It is strong-growing to 20ft (6m) with glossy, leathery, mid-green leaves and puts on a tremendous display of bloom at midsummer. The white, scented flowers, coming in large clusters and opening from yellow buds, have pointed petals, like small stars, but it must be added that they can fade with a slight purplish tinge and can become spotted and streaked after rain. AM 1950.

## Chapter 16
# Climbers

PERHAPS it would be as well to start by defining the difference between a rambler and a climber, as this is a puzzle to many people. Having said this, there comes a pause for reflection. What about the roses that disregard the rules? What about those that seem to come halfway between the two? Am I going to trip myself up by being too precise? Perhaps. We shall see.

In the most general (and cautious) terms, then, climbers have medium-sized to large flowers, usually in smallish clusters, and form a permanent framework of fairly rigid canes, building up from year to year. Pruning consists of shortening the laterals by about two thirds in autumn and the occasional hard cutting back of a main cane or two if the rose becomes bare at the base to encourage new basal shoots. But as a matter of fact, if you would prefer to put your feet up and read a book, by all means do so. Most climbers will be quite happy for many years with no pruning at all except perhaps for the cutting back of a cane or two which is preventing you from seeing out of the window. The book you choose to read should not, needless to say, be one on how to prune climbers.

Most, though not all, climbers are remontant.

When a rose has the word 'Climbing' added before or after its variety name in a list or catalogue (or in this book), it means that it is a climbing sport of what was originally a bush variety. In other words a bush of that variety has for no immediately discernible reason – except perhaps to a botanist – developed the long canes of a climber, and once this has happened it can be propagated from and more climbers produced from it. Some care should, however, be taken in choosing climbing sports because the majority have a very poor second flowering and some, wonderfully remontant in bush form, do not repeat at all. A number of nurseries are dropping them from their catalogues now that so many good, new and really remontant climbers are being produced, though the climbing sports served their turn at a time when breeding of new varieties seemed almost to have come to a standstill.

Despite all this, you will find a few of them included in the descriptions of roses that follow. There are several reasons for this. In the first place there are some climbing sports that do repeat. In the second a number of them are varieties not to be missed despite their poor second showing and that not only blend in with the old garden roses but put on a display at midsummer that few of any sort can match. And thirdly, one or two are climbing forms of Tea roses, and this is the only way in which all but a limited number of these can be expected to survive in anything other than a really warm and mild climate. So you can at least sample a few of their delights.

And now I want to mention something which is based on my own experience, but which I know is doubted by others who would certainly seem to know just as much about it as I do. Most people agree that one should not prune any climber for the first year or two. They are usually slow to get going and best left to their own devices but, and here we come to it, I think that it is especially risky to cut back a climbing sport. Reversion to bush form has happened in my garden as a result of this before I knew that it was a possibility – or that climbers should not be cut back anyway. However, as both kinds of directive involve an idea that is always welcome – that one should do nothing at all – I need hardly say more about it.

In this chapter, except where they consort particularly well with the old garden roses because of their flower form or colouring, I have concentrated on the older climbers, a number of which were contemporaries of roses of the nineteenth century. They have their own kind of charm which a good many of the newcomers lack, but if you do want something more modern a number of semi-climbers can be found in the Modern Shrub Roses chapter. These are the in-betweens, which make equally good short climbers or lax, free-standing shrubs. They could appear here or where I have put them with equal justification. Many of the German roses produced by Wilhelm Kordes, 'Dortmund' and 'Maigold' being examples, come into this category as I mentioned earlier.

**Alister Stella Gray** Gray, 1894. A long-time favourite, growing to 15ft (4.5m), with its small clusters of orange-yellow buds that open into small, creamy-yellow and richly fragrant flowers. So here, almost needless to say, we start off with a climber with small flowers, which must be exasperating to anyone trying to make sense of the rose family for the first time. Views conflict as to whether 'Alister Stella Gray' repeats well and personally I have only seen it at midsummer with anything that could be called a real display. That great authority, Graham Thomas, describes it as having 'huge new shoots with large heads of bloom in the autumn' and as it is a great favourite of his he should know. Looks particularly fine against an old, mellowed, brick wall.

**Allen Chandler** Chandler, 1923. 'Hugh Dickson' × unnamed seedling. A tough, vigorous rose which will reach 15ft (4.5m) or so on a wall and has handsome, dark green leaves. The huge (5in or 13cm) single to semi-double, bright velvety-crimson flowers with their golden stamens are truly spectacular, opening in early summer and continuing to appear with considerable freedom in clusters of three or four throughout the summer. They will be helped in this by the removal of the early orange-red hips – if you can get at them. RNRS GM.

**Altissimo** Delbard-Chabert, 1966. 'Tenor' × unknown variety. Not an old rose by any means, but one of great distinction and similar to a shorter-growing 'Allen Chandler'. As it is unlikely to top 8ft (2.4m) it is very suitable for a pillar or low wall and can also be grown as a lax, free-standing shrub. The 5in (13cm) crimson-red single flowers with their golden stamens come freely and continuously throughout the season, backed by healthy, matt, dark green leaves. RNRS C of M 1965.

*R. banksiae lutea* Not a wild rose, despite its Latin name, but one of a group introduced from China in 1824 and clearly of cultivated origin. It is named in the West after the wife of Sir Joseph Banks. There are several white forms and one other yellow one, R. *banksiae lutescens*, which have single flowers. I have picked out for description the one I think the most attractive, which is the double yellow form. The small, globular, bright yet somehow soft yellow flowers come in large clusters very early in the year and make a wonderful show, but it does need plenty of space because it will easily reach 25ft (7.6m) and is freely branching. Deep, rich soil is best for it and also a warm south-facing wall, otherwise the new shoots, which form one year and flower the next, may well be killed by frost. No pruning should be attempted or you will lose them that way instead. Almost thornless, the canes bear light green, glossy leaves which will remain in place until well into the winter. AM 1960.

**Cécile Brunner, Climbing** 1904. It is worth stressing that this is a climbing sport of the bush variety and *not* 'Bloomfield Abundance', which is sold in place of it more often than it should be. They are quite distinct, not least because, despite the small stature of the original, 'Climbing Cécile Brunner' will easily reach 20ft (6m) or so, sending out huge new canes each year. The very healthy, red-tinted and rather pointed leaves are larger than on the bush form and remain until well into the winter, and the typical very small pink flowers come in large and small clusters with incredible profusion early on. Later there will be some more, but no attempt is made to match the earlier display. See Pl. 10.

**Céline Forestier** Trouillard, 1842. One of a group of climbers with Musk and China rose parentage that originated in America but was largely developed in France – the Noisettes. This one needs some protection – a warm wall or corner – but is a very rewarding variety to grow when once established in conditions it likes, and it is not too vigorous. 8ft (2.4m) or so will be its maximum and it will flower continuously, carrying its small, silky, very double, pale orange-yellow blooms singly and in clusters. The colour in the centre of the blooms is deeper and the scent can be compared to that of a Tea rose. Light green, rather pendulous leaves.

**Desprez à Fleurs Jaunes** Desprez, 1830. 'Blush Noisette' × R. × *odorata ochroleuca*. Also known as 'Jaune Desprez'. The 2in (5cm) double flowers, creamy-yellow with peach and pink tints, have a scent which pervades the air for yards around and are carried continuously throughout the summer on side shoots growing from the robust and well-branched canes. Few thorns, and attractive light green leaves. At its best on a sunny, sheltered wall as its hardiness is slightly suspect, and be prepared for a spread of 18ft (5.5m) or so. A real treasure.

**Elegance** Brownell, 1937. 'Glenn Dale' × ('Mary Wallace' × 'Miss Lolita Armour'). Very vigorous to about 15ft (4.5m) and covered in early summer with large and beautifully shaped primrose-yellow blooms, the colour deeper in the heart of the flower and paler towards the petal edges. Long stems make them ideal for cutting for the house and they will last about two days in water. A little black spot and rather more mildew can be a problem on the mid-green, semi-glossy foliage after the flowers have gone, but despite this it is one of the loveliest of climbers.

**Gloire de Dijon** Jacotot, 1853. A Tea rose × 'Souvenir de la Malmaison'? This old climber has a number of distinctions. It is one of the earliest of all into flower in late spring, and from then on it is more continuously in bloom than almost any other rose, old or new. It is also historically one of the very earliest roses with flowers approaching the modern style to have distinct yellowish tones, though actually it is more buff than yellow with a touch also of apricot. The 4in (10cm) blooms are very double but nobody could, I think, call them very shapely, though some are quartered and all of them are sweetly scented. On a wall it will reach 15ft (4.5m) and does not need pruning. If it gets out of hand, as it may, or if it gets bare at the base, the stoutest canes can be shortened to 6–8ft (1.8–2.4m) and it will soon bush out once more. Certain stock of this rose is said to be deteriorating, which makes it important to buy from a good nursery if you want to make sure of the best plants.

**Golden Showers** Lammerts, 1956. 'Charlotte Armstrong' × 'Captain Thomas'. I have doubts about putting this comparative youngster in with these much older climbers, but as it is equally good as a free-standing shrub it must be found a place somewhere, and so here it is. It is bright yellow, fading after a while to creamy-yellow, seems to be disease-free and really does stay in bloom all summer. There are two main flushes, but there will also be flowers in between, coming from long, elegant buds and opening with not a great many petals to about 4in (10cm) across. They stand up well to rain and, growing on practically thornless stems, are good for cutting and last well. The leaves are dark green and glossy. 8ft (2.4m) is the height usually given, which indicates a pillar for support, but my one on a wall has gone way beyond this. As a shrub it stays erect and makes a good tall hedge, with the advantage that the flowers do not all come at the top. See Pl. 16.

**Lady Hillingdon, Climbing** Lowe and Shawyer, 1910. 'Papa Gontier' × a 'Madame Hoste' sport. The parentage and date given is that of the Tea rose from which this sported in 1917 and it is one of the few Tea roses that is reasonably hardy in anything other than a warm climate. Just the same, it will do better on a warm wall, where it will make a beautiful and robust plant with ruby-red young wood and dark, shiny leaves, purple-tinted when young. It will go up to about 15ft (4.5m) and the long, elegant buds open to soft apricot-yellow, scented flowers, rather loosely formed and nodding, so that they can be seen, appropriately for a climber, to their best advantage from below. Very continuous throughout the summer and well on into the autumn. See Pl. 16.

**Lawrence Johnston** ('Hidcote Yellow') Pernet-Ducher, introduced by Sunningdale Nurseries. 'Madame Eugène Verdier' × R. *foetida persiana*. One of the early Pernetiana roses, not thought worth putting on the market by its raiser, but rescued by others, who proved how wrong he was. It makes a very vigorous climber up to 20ft (6m) and will soon cover the wall of a house. The bright green, glossy leaves set off well the bright yellow flowers which are of medium size and cupped when newly open. After a while they fade slightly and lose some of their shape, but without sacrificing attraction. Only occasionally will there be any of the scented blooms after the first flush. AM 1948.

**Madame Alfred Carrière** Schwartz, 1879. Parents unknown, but generally considered a Noisette. The massed, loosely cupped, medium-sized double flowers, white with a hint of cream or blush, go well with both old and modern roses, and this is a climber that does not mind a north wall. There is a very good display early, spasmodic blooming thereafter, and I have seen flowers on it not many weeks before Christmas. Sweetly scented, it grows up to 25ft (7.6m) and has light but rather dull green leaves, more rounded in shape than usual. It thrives on neglect as I can, rather guiltily, prove, and you can forget about the pruning. See Pl. 16.

**Madame Caroline Testout, Climbing** Pernet-Ducher, 1890. 'Madame de Tartas' × 'Lady Mary Fitzwilliam'. The climbing sport, which is what we are concerned with here, was introduced by Chauvry in 1901 and its robust, thorny canes will take it to 20ft (6m) on a wall if you get the right strain. There are, regrettably, some about that are not so vigorous, as in the case of 'Gloire de Dijon'. The leathery dark leaves may need spraying against mildew, but the first flush of bloom makes any effort worthwhile. It is of the greatest profusion, the individual flowers large, globular and in a soft, clear pearl-pink (not, in fact, unlike the blooms of the first Hybrid Tea, 'La France'), but they do not have very much scent. After a rest there should be a further but much less prolific blooming.

**Madame Grégoire Staechelin** ('Spanish Beauty') Dot, 1927. 'Frau Karl Druschki' × 'Château de Clos Vougeot'. Having used up all my superlatives I am at a bit of a loss, but I do not think I have, on reflection, yet used breathtaking about a climber. That is certainly the right word for the display this rose puts on over many weeks in late spring, unmatched I would say by any other climbing rose, though it will not come again. The sheer quantity of its 5in (13cm), clear pink, loosely semi-double flowers, which show a darker pink on the reverse of the petals, must be seen to be believed. All 20ft (6m) of it will be covered with them and with fine dark leaves. Often suggested for a north wall, though I have no experience to bear this out. Cut back one or two old canes vigorously when it gets bare at the base. See Pl. 16.

**Meg** Gosset, 1954. 'Paul's Lemon Pillar' × 'Madame Butterfly'. If one wanted to choose a rose to illustrate the unpredictability of rose breeding one need go no further than 'Meg'. On one side a climber with enormous, globular, double flowers; on the other a Hybrid Tea which actually has quite small flowers for the type, but ones that are double and perfectly formed, with high, conical centres. And here is 'Meg' with very large, semi-double flowers which open flat, a mixture of pink and apricot, and flaunting their amber stamens. They come in early summer and keep on for many weeks, followed by large but not showy hips. Some say that if these are removed there will be more bloom later, but never having removed them I cannot confirm this. I have my doubts, however, for most roses that are at all that way inclined will show at least a token of a second flowering, even if the hips are left on, and with me 'Meg' never has. The strong dusky-red canes will reach 15ft (4.5m). The large, dark green, semi-glossy leaves are not proof against mildew, especially on soft new growth. RNRS GM 1954.

**Mermaid** W. Paul, 1918. R. *bracteata* × a double yellow Tea rose. This is a climber about which I have mixed feelings, though I am aware that I am in the minority over this. It is certainly almost always in flower from late midsummer onwards and each individual bloom (they come in clusters) is a thing of extreme beauty, but for me there are only rarely enough of them at one time. A climbing rose should be, I feel, something for mass effect, since one cannot appreciate the details of each flower when they are 6ft (1.8m) or more from the ground. They are large, single, and sulphur-yellow, deepening towards the centre where there is a fine show of amber stamens, which persist after the petals have fallen. You buy the plant growing in a pot and very tiny it seems when it arrives, for it does not take kindly to moving when it has reached any size. This means, of course, that you have to wait longer than usual for it to achieve its eventual 20–30ft (6–9m), for it will become a real monster, with deadly, hooked prickles, though a sheltered wall is advised as it is not always completely hardy. Strong as they appear, the canes are apt to snap off from the main stems unless care is exercised when training. I have always followed the injunction that it resents pruning. The result with my specimen is that, due to shade from some beech trees on the side of the house where it is growing, it has gone up and up and there are no leaves or flowers at all for the first 15ft (4.5m). Just bare stems, which I have disguised to some extent with evergreen shrubs and 'Climbing Cécile Brunner' trained as horizontally as possible. However, as 'Mermaid' is shortly about to obscure the bedroom windows, I have decided to ignore all advice and give it a really tough going over this winter. If this book should ever go into a second edition, I will promise you the results. The shiny foliage is almost evergreen and seems to be proof against all disease.

**Mrs Herbert Stevens, Climbing** McGredy, 1910. 'Frau Karl Druschki' × 'Niphetos'. The climbing sport was introduced by Pernet-Ducher in 1922. A robust old climber that will reach 20ft (6m), with good foliage (a very important asset with a climber or rambler), though I have seen mildew and black spot on it late in the season. Exquisite pointed buds opening to long-petalled double flowers in creamy-white with just a touch of green, scented and remontant, but not very happy in prolonged rain. Long stems for cutting if you get at it before the raindrops. See Pl. 16.

**New Dawn** Somerset Rose Nurseries, 1930. A sport of the once-flowering rambler, 'Dr W. Van Fleet', has resulted in this, a first-rate remontant climber, but rambler sports have a habit of doing strange things, as will have been gathered, or should have been gathered, from the descriptions of a number of other roses in this book. It has a fine second flush and some flowers in between as well, but it is not quite as vigorous as the parent rose and will not go much over 10ft (3m), enough for many gardens nowadays. The small to medium-sized, fragrant, blush-pink blooms are produced in clusters with tremendous freedom. The leaves are dark green and glossy and healthy as a rule, though they can get a touch of mildew. Good as a pillar rose or for draping over a low wall.

**Paul's Lemon Pillar** Paul, 1915. 'Frau Karl Druschki' × 'Maréchal Niel'. The lemon is only discernible at the heart of the huge, very full blooms, which are to all intents and purposes white and which, considering the number of petals, do very well in wet weather. In comparison with most climbers it is late in coming into flower, but it is then covered over a long period with its shapely blooms in clusters of three or four. The petals drop cleanly and are followed by enormous hips, but these stay green and are not easily seen against the dark green matt foliage, which may be attacked by mildew late in the season. Despite its name, I have found it much too vigorous for any pillar other than that of a Greek temple, and it should really be trained as horizontally as is possible, for it is a rose that rarely if ever sends up new shoots from the base, preferring to branch higher up. It will reach 10–15ft (3–4.5m) in time. See Pl. 16.

**Sombreuil, Climbing** Robert, 1850. 'Gigantesque' seedling. Classified as a Tea rose (even though 'Gigantesque' was a Hybrid

Perpetual), sometimes as a bush rose and sometimes as a climber, this is a bit of a puzzle. I have seen it grown both ways and certainly as a climber it is only moderately vigorous, perhaps reaching 10ft (3m), and very suitable for a warm corner of a small garden because it usually needs protection except in a very mild climate. The large and very double flowers with their short centre petals open flat and sometimes quartered, ivory-white with flesh tints at the heart and a typical Tea rose scent. Something for all the senses except hearing. See Pl. 16.

**Zéphirine Drouhin** Bizot, 1868. Famous as the 'thornless rose', this is a Bourbon climber, very robust and hardy. It will grow anywhere, is easy to train, and is useful for pillar, fence, pergola, wall or arch; with some support it will even make a hedge. Reaching a height of about 15ft (4.5m), it has light green leaves, coppery when young, which are, unfortunately, almost certain to fall prey to mildew. The vivid cerise-pink of the loosely double, 3in (7.5cm), fragrant flowers gives a spectacular display in early summer (particularly if rain keeps away), and though the rose is certainly remontant, do not expect too much of it later on. The early showing may raise too many hopes.

## Chapter 17

# Getting the Best Out of Them

THERE is a world of difference between deciding that you are going to grow a single shrub rose, which is how most people start out and how I began, and deciding to grow a collection of them, which is how most people finish up once they have had a taste of them. A single rose can quite easily be placed according to its size and colour, though it is as well to know just where you intend to put it before you buy. Many is the time I have poked about trying to find an adequate spot in which a shrub I have bought on impulse will have to sit for the rest of its life, and this is not very sensible. It should not have to keep its arms rigidly to its sides for ever if it is of the sort that likes to make expansive gestures, which means it is important to know to what size it is likely to grow.

So even for a single rose at least some preliminary thought is needed, but a collection is a very different matter. One really has to tax the brain so that a garden will end up with all the parts in harmony, rather than as a kind of Irish stew. This means that some real planning will be needed, even if it is only in your head, if you are to avoid moving your roses about in a yearly musical chairs because they were badly placed to begin with. Such moves may not do a rose any permanent harm, but each time it will suffer a setback and so take that much longer to achieve what you are aiming for.

To get it absolutely right first time would be the work of a genius and mistakes will inevitably be made. Learning from them is one of the attractions of adventurous gardening, and there will be times, too, when one is forced into a change because a rose which the books (including this one) say should reach only shoulder-height is found to be pushing twice that or more after a few years for no discernible reason. There is nothing one can do about the problem except move the rose or its neighbours, but actual mistakes can be minimised, not only by planning out the site and reading

books, but by doing something which I will now mention for the
first time and may refer to several times more, so important is it:
namely to see the varieties you would like to buy growing in
another garden, fully established and over a complete season. It
may not be quite so important to do this if you are timidly
venturing a single China rose or Polyantha, or even – greatly
daring – two of each, but for any rose that you have reason to
believe will reach 5ft (1.5m) or more, this really is the wisest thing
to do. More and more rose nurseries are carrying at least a limited
stock of shrub roses, sometimes container-grown, and it is all too
tempting when wandering round to fall for something which in its
container may be no more than a dainty 18in (45cm) tall but which,
once planted and away, will envelop you like a thorny octopus
each time you venture into the garden. I shall deal in the final
chapter with where you can go to see all of the roses fully grown,
and even if going to see them involves something of a journey it
will be a rewarding one. You may even discover roses new to you
and of undreamt-of beauty, and completely change your plans as a
result, making the trip one of what might be described as joyous
frustration. Back, as Peter Arno might have said, to the old
nursery lists.

Is it best to make a selection of the roses one likes and then fit
them into the garden one has without making any radical changes?
One can do this, of course, and it is certainly the easy way out. It
depends, naturally, on how far you want to go, but as a beginning
go out of your front or back door and, according to the size of
your garden, either look at it in its entirety or else stroll round it.
Ask such questions as, does that hideous shed, your own or the
one next door, need something to hide it? How about replacing
that dull privet hedge with something that will be a mass of bloom
for five or six months? Could that rather dreary path be livened by
a specimen rose planted at the end of it to give some sort of focal
point where it widens out? Would a rose arch distract the eye
upwards from the muddy morass one has to walk through to reach
the vegetable garden, combined with, preferably, adding some
paving stones under foot while you are about it? Or growing
rather more expansive, what about a pergola to lead you down to
the lake? Or that broad bed against the wall: roses in graded
heights with a climber or two behind them would look wonderful
there, and that old rough bank with grass too coarse even for a

mower to chew needs something done about it. Then a glance over the shoulder may reveal to you for the first time, or reinforce a feeling that you have had for years, that your house could really be called rather Pecksniffian, and badly needs something to disguise the fact. And finally, can we give a little parasitic glamour to that ancient holly tree? Better that than trying to grub it out.

Such thoughts, serious and not so serious, should be going through your mind, and if you have done at least a little homework the answers should come out pat. For the shed, something like 'Rambling Rector'. For the hedge, Rugosas, Hybrid Musks, or 'Queen Elizabeth' if space is at a premium. For the end of the path, 'Frühlingsgold', 'Nevada', R. × *alba maxima*, 'Golden Wings' or a weeping standard. For the rose arch, a rambler or climber and for the pergola the same but multiplied according to its length. For the broad bed, small Gallicas at the front, rising to Damasks or Bourbons or both, backed by climbers. For the bank, trailing roses of the Macrantha group or else R. × *paulii*. For the house, any bushy roses that will not completely smother the air-bricks and above them climbers once more. And finally for the holly, 'Complicata', 'Climbing Cécile Brunner' or a Musk rambler.

There are endless other suggestions that one could make as the possible permutations are, like the characters of the different roses, almost limitless. If you wish completely to redesign your garden, I cannot really be of great help to you, because it is impossible to do this without seeing it and, very important, its surroundings. Each garden presents its own problems and there is no formula that will fit every one, but if you have decided to start the whole thing from scratch a number of the suggestions given above and also in what follows may well be of use. For the moment we will continue with adaptation, and having established a principle of working, a *modus operandi* (just to keep our hand in with the Latin), it may be helpful to examine the situations which have been discussed briefly, and a number of others as well, in more detail. We will take something quite simple to start with: the choice and siting of a specimen rose.

Beginning with one used as a focal point at the end of a path, it is essential that the path be wide enough or else that it opens out at the end into a circle or oval. Alternatively it could be placed where another path crosses the first one, but the vital thing is that there must be space both for the rose and for you to get past it – when it is fully grown. A weeping standard in such a spot might be just the answer because it will be reasonably circumspect and controllable, whereas roses such as 'Frühlingsgold' or R. *moyesii*, with their immensely long and flexible, arching canes, would, when the winter winds were blowing, stand there like a circus ringmaster with twenty whips. Nothing beats either of these two, of course, for specimen planting, but the centre of a lawn is a much more suitable place for them.

Then one has to decide whether to choose a once-flowering or remontant variety, and this will depend on several factors. I have already touched on this point, and the fact that some roses are not at their best once the blooms have faded is especially important to take into account with one that is standing all on its own, and even more so if your garden is small. In this case there is no doubt that a remontant modern shrub rose, or perhaps one of the Bourbons or a climber on a pillar, is the best thing.

If you decide that you do not much mind no second flowering and want to use one of the species, remember that a number of them come into bloom very early in the year when there may be rain and icy winds buffeting your garden. The fireside (or space-heater) acts like a magnet and you do not want to venture out, so do not tuck the roses away, out of sight from the windows. If they can be against a background of dark evergreens, so much the better, for the tangled twigs of deciduous shrubs behind them will diffuse and lessen their impact enormously.

One further place for a specimen is the centre of a circular or oval bed to give it height, surrounding it with other roses or else different plants altogether. Something really upright and compact is needed so that the minimum of shadow is cast and the rose does not reach out in time and smother its neighbours. Again, a pillar rose will answer very well, or else a standard. Provided that the colour does not cause problems, and it is difficult to imagine it clashing with anything, the shrub rose 'Ballerina' would be an unbeatable choice for such a spot in almost any garden as it makes a fine, big, but not too overpowering, head in standard form. Avoid a weeping standard which, apart from being likely to flower once only, will need a lot of space left round it. Its whippy canes will eventually hang down to the ground and could cause a lot of damage to surrounding plants if blown about in the wind. Tying them in would be no answer. For their full effect, they should hang as freely as nature (or rather man, for there are no standards in nature) intended.

Moving on from specimens to hedges, which to many of us mean something that has to be clipped at least once a year to keep it spruce and tidy. Such hedges have their place, and a thick evergreen barrier may be a necessity, perhaps to act as a windbreak or to divert cold air that might otherwise roll down a slope to form a frost pocket at the bottom. An evergreen such as a holly will also form a screen to give privacy all the year round, which no rose can do. So, too, will cupressus, those refugees from cemeteries whose funereal dullness seems to be blighting every garden in the land, and whose only attraction is that they grow quickly, as often as not to three or four times the height envisaged when they were planted. But need a hedge be either dull or formal or both? Indeed it need not.

It should be as gay and colourful as any other part of a garden, and this is just what roses can make it. Old and modern shrub roses can provide hedges ranging from 8ft (2.4m) or so high – enough for most people – down to about 3ft (1m), if something as low as that can still be called a hedge. They can be both thorny and extremely dense if one of the Rugosa family is used, such as 'Roseraie de l'Hay', with beautiful bright green leaves from which not only the common rose diseases shy away, but for some strange reason greenfly as well. Plant them about 4–5ft (1.2–1.5m) apart and after a few years, for they are fast-growing, they will form a barrier that a charging knight in full armour would swing his steed away from. If he snatched a bloom for his lady as he passed, he would be sucking the prickles from his fingers for a long time afterwards.

Among other unbeatable hedging roses are the Hybrid Musk group of shrub roses. While these may well be more spectacular in bloom even than the Rugosas, they will also be a great deal less regular in shape and more open and unpredictable in their habit of growth. If one wants to consider mixing the varieties some caution is needed, because there can be quite a variation in size between the different ones. 'Cornelia', 'Penelope', 'Prosperity', 'Pink Prosperity' and 'Felicia' are all much of a muchness, but the taller 'Vanity', and 'Moonlight' at its best, could easily look odd men out. So, too, at the other end of the scale, could 'Danaë'.

One thing that you must be prepared for with both these rose families is width as well as height. 5ft (1.5m) or more must be allowed, and though with the Rugosas a certain amount of light trimming back in winter can be done without ill effects, this will not substantially reduce the overall size. Some pruning can be carried out with the Hybrid Musks, though they are far better if left to grow free and unrestrained. Alternatively, they can be formed into a hedge no more than 3ft (1m) wide by tying them in to horizontal wires or chain-link mesh strung between strong wooden uprights. This tying in must be done right from the very beginning or the strong flowering branches, left to themselves, will certainly shoot out sideways and be difficult or impossible to bring under control again without damaging them beyond repair or even snapping them off altogether. It would certainly be a pity to have to remove them intentionally, so fairly regular tying in of shoots that develop later will be needed.

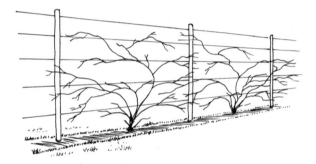
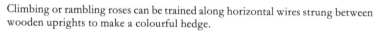

Climbing or rambling roses can be trained along horizontal wires strung between wooden uprights to make a colourful hedge.

The same kind of post and wire structure can be used as the foundation for a hedge of climbing or rambling roses, keeping the canes as near to the horizontal as possible to encourage side shoots low down. While such a hedge can be even taller than one formed from shrub roses alone, it will be extremely difficult to make it into a dense screen. If its purpose is purely decorative, there is nothing that will look more lovely or be more colourful, but almost inevitably there will be gaps in it at varying heights where there is a shortage of suitably placed canes to train across them. Planting the climbers or ramblers at 5–6ft (1.5–1.8m) intervals, closer than you would otherwise do so that the canes of one will overlap and interweave with those on each side, will be a considerable help, but before finalising the planting distances some account must be taken of the vigour and bushiness of the roses you are using. 'Pink Perpétue' would need closer planting than 'Mermaid'.

For late summer flowers when the climbers may be resting or the ramblers have finished their display, grow clematis up through them, preferably one of the blues, which will make a wonderful combination with white, pale yellow or buff roses, especially if at least part of the flowering periods of the two overlap. Choose your clematis from the late-flowering Viticella group, which should be cut back hard in early spring each year so that you avoid ending up with an impenetrable tangle of old growth that will gradually overwhelm the roses in its boa-constrictor embrace.

For hedges of a more modest height and width there are the Gallicas – though a warning about a possible drawback these have is given in the Gallica chapter – and numerous shrub roses that are either Floribundas in disguise such as 'Chinatown' or 'Angelina' or a shrub rose pure and simple such as 'Sally Holmes' or 'Golden Wings'. Down the scale – even below 3ft (1m) – there is 'Ballerina' or 'The Fairy' or 'Yesterday', and right up at the other end, modest in width if not in height, is 'Queen Elizabeth'. Its entry in the Modern Shrub Roses chapter gives details of how to get the best out of this one for hedging, and with both it, and rather less so with 'Chinatown', staggered planting is worth considering to give density low down.

*Ground-cover*

Of recent years the use of ground-cover plants has been talked and written about *ad nauseum*. It has value, yes, but certainly not to the extent that some writers imply. It is not the be-all and end-all, and it is equally certain that it is not, as one might think, a new idea. Nature has been covering the ground with a carpet of plants since time began, and if you leave a piece of bare earth for a few weeks the hoof-beats of a charge of ground-elder or couch-grass will be heard loud and clear. But that, to be fair, is not what gardeners mean by ground-cover. We like to dictate what goes where, and I would say that ground-cover plants are not the best things to use with roses, except perhaps at the very edges of the beds. There are other plants that can be grown among them – these will be dealt with a little later on – but the kinds that form a dense carpet of foliage can seriously interfere with the proper cultivation of the roses, rob the soil on a massive scale of the food intended for them, and make such things as pruning and spraying very difficult. It is much better to use a mulch, which can do nothing but good, even though birds, and especially blackbirds, will certainly scatter much of it over lawns or paths surrounding the beds as if they were giving it away to the poor. Either get an airgun, a cat, or preferably just sigh and sweep the mulch back on the beds again.

The use of roses themselves as ground-cover plants to keep weeds down is another matter, and also one about which I have certain reservations.

I recently spent a tiring morning with a friend working among a mixed planting of R. ×paulii, R. ×paulii rosea and 'Max Graf', all three varieties recommended for ground-cover, with which in time my friend is hoping to cover completely a very wide and rough grass bank. I, too, hope that he succeeds because it is being done on my recommendation, but the roses have now been there for about four years and have only reached about half their ultimate size. This means that they have formed dense, low thickets about 6–7ft (1.8–2.1m) across, and my job on this occasion was, using a long-handled rake because of the unbelievably dagger-like thorns, to hold up the long canes that were questing out across the ground like the spokes of a wheel and were half hidden in the surrounding grass. In time these, too, will mound themselves up as the centre of the bush has already done, and all the grass will be smothered, but in the meantime my friend wanted to tidy things up. As I held up the canes, he ran his mower under them and the job was done, but I hope it will be realised by now that I am recounting this to make a point. In another few years the whole bank will, as I say, be covered by the roses – perhaps less thoroughly so by 'Max Graf' than the others – and at midsummer will be one solid mass of bloom in two tones of pink and white, but in planning to use roses in this way time and patience must be built into one's plans. This was, of course, an exceptionally big bank, and with a smaller one coverage would have been completed more quickly. I would then have been helping in the trimming back of canes that wanted to go further afield rather than holding them up, but even so, whatever the size of the bank or other spot in which these roses may be planted, during the first few years weeding between the developing canes, or else cutting the grass which grows up through them, will still be needed, with strong leather gloves an absolute necessity. Ground-cover roses are not, in other words, an instant answer.

*Pegging down*

For the actual mechanics of this you will have to read the chapter on Practical Care, but here it can be said that it is a way of getting the best out of roses such as many of the Hybrid Perpetuals, which send up long yet reasonably flexible canes with flowers perched precariously only at the very tips. It can also be used to get what might be described as the better than best out of any long-caned rose, Bourbons and the like, and even some climbers being used as shrubs, for it will increase the number of flowers enormously. It involves bending the canes over gently in winter rather than shortening them by pruning, and literally pegging the ends down close to the ground. This has the same results as the horizontal training of a climber and dormant buds right along the canes will break into flowering shoots. If the pegging down is done with some sort of system – the canes of one rose meshing with those of the roses next to it – midsummer will bring a carpet of blooms over the whole bed and in winter it will not look like a riverside fishing competition. There will be few long stems for cutting since the flowers will be mostly on short side shoots, but otherwise there will be everything else you could desire. If a wire frame is used over the beds rather than pegs, clematis can be added to the roses, as was suggested for the climbing rose hedge. It does not *have* to grow upwards.

Pegging down, while effective in a big bed, does not have to involve a great many roses. One on its own can be pegged, leaving some of the centre canes (cut back a little) standing upright and only tying down the outer ones, which will give an intriguing crinoline skirt effect. The outer canes, if not too long, and if they will stand it without danger of snapping, can even be bent over and tied in to the base of the plant itself.

*Pillars and tripods*

As both of these are almost essential forms of support for certain kinds of roses, it might be as well to say a brief word about how they differ and why and when one is preferable to the other. Two main factors come into it, the space available and the vigour of the rose, to which one might add how freely branching it is. A pillar is just what the name suggests, straight up and straight down, and made from a roughly squared-off post or else a section of a tree trunk, usually a conifer. With the latter, if stumps of most of the branches, cut to about a foot in length, are left in place there will be that much more to tie the canes of the rose to and they will not be so confined as they would be on a simple pillar.

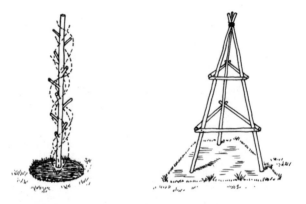

A pillar (*left*) and a tripod for training short climbers or for confining many shrub roses within a reasonable compass. Branch stubs have been left on the pillar for easier tying in. The dotted lines show how the roses should be trained in a spiral round the pillar.

Pillars are best for moderately vigorous climbers and other roses that do not branch with too much abandon. A tripod, which is a kind of wigwam assembled from three or four substantial rustic poles, lashed together at the top and preferably with bracing crosspieces about halfway down the legs, does need more space but can display a comparatively freely branching rose such as a Bourbon much more effectively. With so many components making it up, the canes of the rose can be more fully spread out on

148

a tripod and it will be easier to achieve flowering low down if the canes are wound round at first and only gradually allowed to make their way upwards. This kind of training should also be done with pillar roses, but it will be much more difficult if a variety has stiff and uncooperative canes. The turning circle round a pillar will be that much less than that of a tripod.

*Roses with other plants*

The idea that roses should not be mixed with other plants is a long time in dying, because it probably started in Victorian times. This, as we know from the discussion of the development of flower forms, was the period when rose shows first burst on a waiting world and became enormously popular. It was also the time when a number of rose books were written by a group of rose-loving clergymen, notably Canon Reynolds Hole and the Reverend A. Foster-Melliar, both of whom were dedicated exhibitors. There is no doubt that exhibition roses are best grown in isolation if they are to be given the detailed cultivation programme they need for anything other than a purely local flower show, and it was this sort of thinking that went into the advice both the authors gave. Foster-Melliar was the more single-minded of the two, but as their books went into edition after edition and became standard works on rose gardening, people who would not have thought of showing their roses read them and never considered that there were alternatives if they did not. Somehow the idea has stuck.

One can think of other reasons why the idea has persisted. There is a practical side to isolating roses, not only for shows but for bedding, too. Things such as spraying and mulching are easier if one does not have to consider, for instance, whether a particular chemical spray might damage the leaves of something else, or whether a mulch might smother a smaller plant. In addition, the often compact and rather stiff upright stance of Hybrid Teas and Floribundas does not encourage an informal mingling.

The picture changes, however, when one thinks of the lax and spreading canes of so many of the old roses. A low-growing Damask, a dainty China or wild types such as R. *rubrifolia* will look perfectly in place in a border, whatever else may be there, and as long as colour blending is not forgotten. Or a tall rose such as R. × *alba maxima*, or even two or three of them, with their white

149

flowers and fine, grey-green leaves, would add interest if placed at one end of a bed of other plants. That distinguished gardening writer Brigadier C.E. Lucas Phillips even advocates, and practises, the growing of roses among dwarf rhododendrons, which would certainly give early colour and the attraction of shiny green foliage for the rest of the year, though I would have thought that the ideal growing conditions for the two kinds of plant did not quite coincide.

Speaking for myself, I have a very large bed rather resembling in plan the coast of Greece, with many islands and peninsulas in it, mainly made up of winter-flowering heathers. Shrub roses grow in the sea between the islands, placed so that they do not cast too much shade and rob the heathers of the sun they love. Elsewhere I describe how disastrous this concept turned out to be with one particular kind of rose, but it certainly works for the others. There is evergreen foliage at a lower level than rhododendrons would give and wonderful winter colour as the heather comes into bloom. I have also mentioned the foxgloves that have seeded themselves there, and at one time I had clumps of lilies as well, mainly pink, white and cream, which gave the same kind of contrast with their tall spires of bloom. Unfortunately they did not survive in my poor, dry soil (which is far from ideal for roses, of course), but for those who can grow them they are just the thing.

There are other shrubs in the bed, apart from the heather and roses. A gnarled old bush of rosemary with its blue-green leaves and tiny pale blue flowers, an enormous free-standing *Cytisus battandieri* (Moroccan broom) up which I am training a 'Climbing Cécile Brunner', and in one corner the rambler 'Félicité et Perpétue' is scrambling though a *Buddleia alternifolia*. These and one or two clumps of the grey-leaved shrubby potentillas provide the kind of foliage that goes exceptionally well with roses. For the same effect, I use lavender, nepeta, anaphalis, senecio and *Phlomis fruticosa* elsewhere.

The growing of clematis up through climbing rose hedges we know about, but it can be used just as effectively with roses on a wall, either to add new colour when the roses are out or to provide it when they are over or resting. Other climbing plants can be used as well, such as sweet peas, which are particularly useful with roses that like to show their leafless, flowerless, gnarled old legs. As an alternative, a rose can be grown up through another wall shrub such as ceanothus, which will give you a powdery blue either early or late according to the variety, chaenomeles for early pink blossom, or pyracantha with its gay if not garish autumn display of berries and rather retiring white flowers earlier on.

## The scramblers

If roses such as the Gallica hybrids 'Complicata' or 'Scarlet Fire' want to scramble into something else then let them, or better still encourage them to do so by providing a host shrub nearby or a wall over which they can drape themselves. After all, this is the kind of way most roses grow in the wild and is probably one of the reasons why they are provided with hooked thorns. They are the ice axes of the climber or rambler and on them they can lift themselves from quite dense cover into the light. This means that scrambling or trailing roses can actually be planted in a certain amount of shade, provided always that there is a clear avenue of escape left open for them. A wild rose growing in a hedgerow falls into this category, weaving its way steadily up and out of the tangle at the hedge bottom. It thrives and shows that it is doing so by decorating with its delicate blooms the branches and twigs that support it. Later on hips will come as well, and it is just this natural effect that we are aiming for with the perhaps more sophisticated cultivated varieties.

## A diversion

At this point I am going to divert briefly, in the interests of accuracy, from the subjects we have been discussing. I have been, am doing and will continue to refer to a rose's 'thorns'. This is what they are commonly called, but in strict botanical terms they are no such thing. They are prickles, for thorns do not grow at random from the bark of a shoot as they do on a rose. Thorns, as the dictionary puts it, are aborted branches, springing from a leaf axil or the tips of shoots, as they do on gorse or hawthorn. Generally they are straight, and they must in this case be purely defensive. Gorse and hawthorn do not climb.

Having taken one side road, I may as well take another. In *Shrub Roses for Every Garden* I used the word 'heps' for the fruit of the rose. In this book I am using 'hips', and the question of which is right has in the meantime been the subject of a heated debate. The answer is that they are quite interchangeable and one can use either, but experience has shown that far more people know at once what a hip is. 'Hep' brings a slightly puzzled frown, so it seemed sensible to make the change.

*Chapter 18*

# Practical Care

As far as the information in this chapter is concerned, a certain amount of knowledge of rose growing is going to be assumed. Very few people start straight away with shrub roses, regrettable as this may be, and those that come to them in the course of time generally have some experience with bedding roses. So there will be no treatise on the art of pruning from the very beginning. There will not be a blow-by-blow account of ten rounds with a constantly clogging fungicide spray, or even the A, B and C of the basic points of spraying itself. Instead it seems more sensible to concentrate on those aspects of cultivation that are either peculiar to the kinds of roses we are dealing with, or else that are, though of universal application, of very great importance and need stressing whatever kind of rose you may be growing.

*The site*

The section on soil which follows this one will also give a number of pointers as to the best site for roses, for instance that they should not be grown in a boggy hollow – a rose is not a mangrove. But first of all we must deal with conditions above ground, and the most important thing of all to make sure of is that there is plenty of sunlight. There may be a lack of cooperation in this from the sun itself, but of what little may be going they should have as big a share as possible. Roses grown in the shade will become gaunt and leggy, but apart from this the heat of the sun is needed to ripen the new canes that form each year, so that they can stand up to the frost and icy winds of winter. One has only, after a hard frost, to look at what has happened to a soft and sappy cane that has developed during a dull, damp autumn to see the truth of this. It will be blackened and will die back, so that all the energy that went into producing it will have come to nothing.

So full sun for half of each day at the very least is the main priority for a rose bed, which in most gardens is not too difficult to achieve. However, problems can arise with shrub roses if they are planted amongst other shrubs. It is important to choose as their neighbours ones that will not overwhelm them and cut out the light. If the rose is of a kind that will scramble up through them and reach the sun in its own way, well and good, but otherwise the other shrubs should be on the side away from the sun or very well spaced out. Alternatively they can be of about the same size or smaller than the roses themselves, and though basically it all depends on the relationship of one to another, this is something that it is essential to think out at the very beginning. Otherwise one is faced with moving established bushes about like the guests in an over-booked Egyptian hotel.

A windy site in open, flat country or on a hill top is likely to present a different kind of problem. No rose likes living in a nonstop gale, and all one can say in favour of conditions like this is that it would be unlikely to get either black spot or mildew. The airborne spores which spread both of these from one rose bush to another simply would not be able to grab hold of the leaves as they went whistling past, but freedom from disease, while welcome, would not make up for flowers and leaves dashed to pieces on the long, lax canes of so many of the old roses. And the big and often very tall bushes would be rocked about in the wind and the roots probably loosened in the soil.

A windbreak on the side of the garden from which the prevailing wind comes is the answer – tall evergreen shrubs, for preference of a kind that do not mind a bit of a blow; or if the roses are not too tall, a wattle fence might do, with climbers to hide it. Something is needed through which a certain amount of the wind can pass, slowing down as it does so, because a completely solid barrier can cause its own problems simply by diverting and not slowing down currents of air so that they set up turbulence which can do as much damage as the wind itself. If conditions are not too extreme, the Rugosa family of roses can themselves be used as a windbreak. They are compact growers and extremely tough, even, if they are forced into it, standing up to salt-laden winds from the sea, though the leaves will accept this better than the flowers. But they will not, of course, go much above 5–6ft (1.5–1.8m) at the most and will possibly be substantially less than this in such a tough environment, so that they would not give protection to anything really tall.

Though roses do not like constant winds, they do like to have air circulating through their branches and will be healthier for it, but just the same, they should not be planted in a draughty spot. The kind of place I have in mind can be found in the narrow space between two buildings even if, and this is unlikely, such a position gets plenty of sun. Such a spot often generates its own wind, and what elsewhere may be a light breeze can, when confined between two high walls, suddenly take on the dimensions of a mini-hurricane.

Finally a word about climbers. A sunny wall is the place for these, but quite often in nursery catalogues one sees a note at the end of a variety description that it is especially suitable for a north wall. This information is not likely to be incorrect, but what it omits to say is that the rose – any rose – will do a great deal better on a south-facing one.

## The soil and its preparation

Roses of one sort or another will grow after a fashion in almost anything short of cast iron. Even in very poor dry soils the Rugosas will flourish, but in general one that is not too heavy or too light is best. They are definitely not fond of chalk, though even here I have been told on good authority that Hybrid Perpetuals and R. × macrantha are reasonably tolerant of it. I have no personal experience of this, but I do know that most roses absolutely hate it because it prevents the roots taking up the iron salts they need, so that the foliage yellows and dies. A preparation called sequestered iron, sold under the name Sequestrene, can be watered on to the beds to counter a mild iron deficiency, but with ground that consists of a little soil over more or less solid chalk something more drastic must be done. Short of moving house, the only thing is to dig as large a hole as possible where you are going to put your rose – certainly not less than 18in (45cm) deep and 2–3ft (60cm–1m) across – and fill it with a mixture of chalk-free soil and peat. Some people also line the hole with strong polythene sheet.

The peat added to the soil is to increase acidity, for chalk soils are alkaline and, though they will put up with a great deal, roses are not at their best at the extremes in either direction. They will grow, yes, even if the balance is far from being right, but if something can be done to tip the scales in the right direction, how much happier and more rewarding they will be.

If you can actually see the chalk you will know that your soil is alkaline. Rhododendrons and azaleas thriving in your area will indicate acidity, but if you suspect one or the other and are unsure that you are right, a soil testing kit is cheap to buy and it will have instructions for using it on the package. The acidity or alkalinity of soil is expressed on something called the pH scale, and for roses the ideal pH figure is about 6.5, or slightly on the acid side of the halfway mark. Nitro chalk can be used to increase alkalinity and is safer to use than lime, which it is all too easy to overdo and then almost impossible to undo if you have used too much. Nitro chalk is also a fertilizer that will provide nitrogen, so it has a double purpose, but really, unless you know that things are not as they should be before you start preparing the beds for your roses, for most people soil testing is hardly worthwhile.

Far more important as a rule is how heavy or how light the soil is. I think it was Christopher Lloyd who told in a book of his how roses under his bedroom window thrived on nail clippings dropped there. One of my 'Climbing Cécile Brunner's does equally well on the filter tips of cigarettes I have smoked at mine on sleepless nights. So one is tempted to say that roses will stand for anything, but more seriously, it is of the utmost importance to add organic matter such as well-rotted stable manure or compost to light soils in order to provide food and to hold moisture, not only at planting time but when put on the beds in the form of a mulch at least once a year afterwards. It will be like feeding the Forth Bridge, for it is quite incredible how quickly mulch will vanish into a sandy soil and need replenishing, but this really does have to be done if the roses are to flourish. Both leaf-mould and peat are best avoided because light soil is likely to be acid and they will make it more so, but I will deal with the practice and theory of mulching in more detail a little later on.

I am afraid that there is no alternative if your soil is poorly drained heavy clay other than to dig it deeply to break it up, not only to make it easier for the roots of the roses to penetrate but also to improve drainage. Though roses do like plenty of water they do not like to stand for ever with their feet wet. Peat, manure, compost and even ashes well dug in – or a combination of all four

– will help to improve the soil structure, lightening it and making it more porous. It is the sort of job that will either break your back or else give you a sense of achievement and exhilaration when you have finished it, for you will have prepared a really good future home in which your roses will live happily for many years. You may come in from the garden looking like Magwich, but it will be worth it.

Two final points on soil preparation. First make as sure as you possibly can that you have cleared the site of persistent perennial weeds, particularly those with roots that spread underground. Leave them, even the tiniest piece of root, and later they will come creeping stealthily back, weaving amongst the roots of the roses from where they will shout defiance at you for evermore.

Secondly, prepare the ground early in the autumn, some two or three months before planting time. The soil should be given a chance to settle down again to a natural density, and any air pockets that the digging may have left deep down, which questing roots will not welcome, will have had a chance to fill themselves in. The organic matter you have added will also have begun to break down through the action of the soil bacteria and be absorbed, so that it can begin its proper function that much sooner.

If anyone should feel that I have gone on too long about preparing the ground, should feel daunted by what I have described as being necessary, there will be some comfort for them in the reflection that it only has to be done once. It is a great temptation just to dig holes any old how in a bed that has perhaps not been disturbed for years, push the roses in and hope for the best. You will not get it.

*Planting*

If you know how to plant one kind of rose you know how to plant all of them, more or less, but here are a few special points to bear in mind.

No rose should be planted close in against a wall, especially that of a house. The bricks of the wall itself will absorb moisture from the earth and when they are warmed by the sun will also have a drying effect. If the house has overhanging eaves these are likely to keep rain away from the walls, and just a little further out, directly under the roof edges, there may be an incessant drip of water, saturating the ground for long periods. Not, therefore, on either account, a place for roses, so put them at least 18in (45cm) away, slanting the canes inwards and fanning the roots outwards towards more normal soil conditions. This applies to a rose that is actually going to climb up the wall. Others in the same bed can be even further away.

Much the same can be said with regard to a tree-climbing rose, which should be planted as far away from the trunk as possible. Not, of course, at the other end of the garden, but it does not matter at all if you have to steer the canes towards the trunk on slanting stakes or bamboo canes from a distance of 3–4ft (1–1.2m) away or even more. There will be competition from the tree both for soil foods and water, and its leaves, increasingly so towards the centre, are likely to give unwelcome shelter from the rain. Distance will eventually lend greater enchantment.

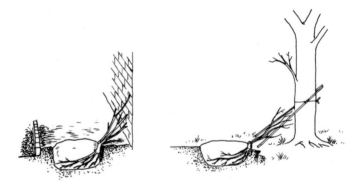

Planting a climbing rose against a wall (*left*) and planting a climber or rambler so that it will climb a tree, showing supporting canes to guide the rose in towards the tree trunk. In both cases the roots are fanned out away from the support towards moister earth.

It will also help in the later stages if a rose is planted on the side of a tree from which the prevailing wind blows. For the first few years you will probably have to tie a number of the canes to convenient branches or the trunk itself, but training will be altogether easier if the wind is blowing them into the tree rather than away from it.

Do not plant standard roses any deeper than is necessary to cover the roots with 3–4in (7.5–10cm) of soil. Most of them are budded on to Rugosa stock and deep planting will encourage it to sucker. You will have young Rugosa suckers (unfortunately of a kind much less attractive than the garden hybrids) popping up like daisies and just as difficult to eliminate. A leafy side shoot on a standard stem should be snapped off as soon as it is seen. The stem itself is part of the rootstock, with the cultivated rose budded on to it at the top, so a shoot on the stem is the same thing in effect as a sucker lower down.

If you are buying container-grown roses, it is just as important as with any other kind to prepare the soil for them as far in advance as possible. For the actual planting, first give the containers a good watering because they will sometimes have dried out. Then dig a hole considerably larger than the container, and when the rose has been placed in this fill in round the root-ball with loosened soil or a planting mixture, treading it reasonably firm afterwards and watering it well. If all you do is dig a small hole into which the root-ball will just fit the soil all round may well be packed tight, and if it is on the heavy side a sump may form after prolonged rain and almost literally drown the rose roots.

Do not plant new roses in a bed that has grown other roses for a number of years. They will not thrive, even though those that may already be there will continue to do so. Nobody seems to know why this should be so, and the best the experts can say about it is that the soil has become rose-sick. It is like your doctor telling you that you have got a virus, but it is impossible to say whether this means that some soil-borne organism is either infecting the roots or else is preventing them from taking up nourishment, or whether it is that the rose, fresh from the rich diet of a nursery, is finding it difficult to cope with the possibly impoverished soil of its new home. Perhaps it is a combination of all three, but it is not sufficient simply to add fertilizer to the old bed. The soil must be replaced to a depth of 3ft (1m) at least – easy to say, and living hell to do – or a new site chosen. For a single rose to replace one that has died in an established bed, dig as large a hole as you can without damaging neighbouring plants and fill it with soil from another part of the garden.

*Pruning summary*

With most of the old rose families you can prune or not, as you wish. Some people do, some do not, but more and better flowers will come if the plants have at least a token going over. Others, particularly some of the modern shrub roses, do need something more, but with each and every one of them remove completely dead or diseased wood as soon as it is seen, summer, autumn, winter or spring.

*Species* This is the one group with which I would agree that no pruning at all should be done, with the exception, possibly, of a little trimming in the early years to achieve a balanced bush. This is especially important if the rose is to form an isolated specimen in a lawn or other place where it can be seen from all sides. Remove dead wood as and when seen.

*Gallicas* Very little pruning needed, but some of them do grow into a thick mass of twiggy shoots that will benefit from being thinned out. They will stand some gentle clipping over in winter if used in a hedge, but the natural outlines of each bush should be followed as closely as possible and no attempt made to force unnatural shaping on them.

*Damasks* Remove twiggy growths after flowering and shorten strong side shoots to encourage the formation of new flowering shoots for the following year. Strong main canes can be cut by up to one third to help increase bushiness.

*Albas* Remove twiggy growth after flowering and shorten the longer remaining shoots by about one third.

*Centifolias* Rather more drastic treatment needed here to try to minimise legginess and encourage branching. The main canes can be reduced by half in winter and side shoots reduced by the same amount.

*Moss roses* As for Centifolias.

*China roses* Little, if any, attention needed, but the shortening of side shoots by about one third in winter may help things along.

*Bourbons* Cut away twiggy wood after flowering and in winter reduce the main shoots by one third. Spur back the remaining side shoots. Bourbons can, of course, be pegged down, or they can be grown on pillars or tripods, in which case only the side shoots will need attention.

*Portlands* As for Bourbons.

*Hybrid Perpetuals* If you peg down, no pruning other than that of a few awkwardly placed shoots and perhaps the spurring back of other longer ones should be needed. Otherwise cut away short, twiggy growth after blooming and shorten main shoots by one third and side shoots to about three eyes. Those that grow like rather tall Hybrid Tea roses – 'Mrs John Laing', for example – can be pruned like them, but not too severely.

*Rugosas* Little pruning except for the tipping back of new growths and, with the more bushy kinds, an occasional fairly drastic thinning out by cutting back a number of the main canes by up to half their length, perhaps removing some of the older ones altogether. As with the Gallicas, they can be clipped over to a limited extent if used for hedging.

*Hybrid Musks* Certainly there will be no shortage of flowers with these, even if you do not prune, but shortening of the side shoots will result in even more. If one of the main canes grows to excessive length so as to unbalance the whole bush or possibly obstruct a path, it can be cut back as hard as is necessary to bring it into line. It will cheerfully set off again when summer comes.

*Polyanthas* Prune as one would a Floribunda.

*Modern shrub roses* Such a diverse group that no general rule will cover them all. As a general guide, prune in the same way as you would any member of the family to which they actually belong, e.g. 'Chinatown', a Floribunda, or that which they closely resemble, e.g. 'Constance Spry', a Bourbon.

*Climbers* These will get along very happily for years with no pruning at all. When it does have to be done, possibly because the rose is taking up too much space, shorten the side shoots by about one third but only cut back the others as much as may be needed to keep them from intruding where they are not wanted. The only time they should be touched otherwise is if the rose is getting bare at the base, when one or two of them cut back really hard should encourage new growth low down.

*Ramblers* For a very long time I have been following long-established convention when writing on the pruning of ramblers. I have advised, as have others before me from time immemorial, the complete removal of the old canes after flowering each year, and the tying-in in their place of the new ones that come up from the base of the plant. Well, this advice is not wrong, but it is a counsel of perfection.

Pruning a rambler on a pillar (*left*). Once the old canes are cut back the new ones are tied in. Climbers (*right*) only need their lateral growths shortened.

It could easily be argued that this is just the sort of counsel that a book like this should give, and while perfectly true in one way, it really ought to be borne in mind that you can get perfectly satisfactory results – certainly good enough for most people's requirements – without doing anything as drastic as is usually suggested. I started to think this out properly when I was looking

162

one day at a rambler 'The Garland' growing up a tree. Nobody in their right mind would, I realised, even think of attempting to disentangle all the old canes so that they could be removed, and in any case why bother to do this with a rose that keeps flowering profusely year after year, as I have seen this one do? From this my thoughts moved on to old cottage gardens, where 'American Pillar' and 'Dorothy Perkins' still drape themselves over walls and arches with unpruned abandon, one mass of flowers each summer, as they have been ever since the day they were planted. From these thoughts I was brought back rather smartly into the present by two embarrassing questions. In the first place, do I always follow the advice I have been giving to others? And if the answer is no – which it is – are my ramblers any the worse for it? Again no.

It is not with me solely (though it may be mainly) a question of laziness, but rather that ramblers should always be grown on openwork supports such as arches, pergolas, trelliswork and so on, and of course up trees. These they will weave through and into until they hardly know their warp from their weft, and getting the old canes out of such a tangle is, if not actually impossible, the kind of job about which, every morning, one should make a fresh resolution to do tomorrow.

I am not, however, advocating that ramblers should never be pruned, so those who treat any rose they are pruning as if a cobra were coiled round it should temper their elation. Some cutting out of the worst of the tangles should be attempted when flowering is over, together with the spurring back of any accessible side shoots. Now and again a main cane obviously on its last legs will have to be got rid of completely, but it may be easier (a strictly relative term in this context) to cut it out in sections rather than try to untie it from its supports as a whole.

Well, I have made a confession, but it is one that has, I hope, also made a point. There are no absolutely hard and fast rules in gardening. If something does not seem quite right for you, or does not work as it should, or even, when you come to think it out, seems rather silly, try something else. All I hope is that you will be quicker off the mark than I was.

## Dead-heading

Not a great deal to say here. Remontant roses will benefit from dead-heading to keep the flowers coming, though many do reasonably well without it. This is fortunate, because with some of the bigger shrubs it may be virtually impossible, short of hiring a gantry to work from. An orang-utan on a stepladder might manage it, but they don't grow roses much.

Dead-heading. Cut to a firm, healthy bud 4–5in (10–12.5cm) below the old flower head.

Always cut to a healthy bud not far below the old flower head, rather than simply pulling the old flowers off. This will ensure that a strong new shoot will grow from the bud. Dead-heading of once-flowering roses is not needed except for the removal with certain varieties of the corpse-like spent blooms when the petals have not been properly shed – decorations for Dracula's Christmas tree. Provided that it has not just rained, a good shaking of the branches will often get rid of a good many of them.

One does not, needless to say, dead-head a rose that is being grown at least in part for its decorative hips.

## Mulching

A mulch is best put on in late spring when the soil has warmed up a little. There are many reasons for mulching: it smothers weeds; it keeps the soil temperature reasonably even; it cuts down moisture loss through evaporation; and, if it is of a suitable organic material,

164

it will break down and provide food for the roses, a process which is speeded up if it is lightly hoed in in the autumn. Well-rotted stable manure or compost are the best food providers, well-rotted because any rotting down process absorbs vast quantities of nitrogen. Roses need nitrogen, too, and if the rotting down took place in or on the earth the compost or manure and the rose roots would be fighting tooth and nail for what was going, with the likelihood that the roses would lose. Horticultural grade peat can be used as a mulch, and though it has no food value, it will carry out the other necessary functions and makes a neat-looking – if fabulously expensive – rose bed. In my experience, about twice as much as you have calculated for will be needed to give a reasonable covering of 2in (5cm) or so, and it does have the disadvantage that when it dries out it becomes very light and can blow about. Pulverised bark looks just as good, is less mobile in a wind, at the present time at least is not so expensive, and has been tried out with great success in the gardens of the Royal National Rose Society at St Albans in Hertfordshire.

*Pegging down*

This, it will be remembered, is a form of training that encourages side shoots on roses with long and reasonably flexible canes which otherwise would flower mainly at the top. The words 'reasonably flexible' are important because the canes do have to be arched over until their tips are only about 6in (15cm) from the ground or even less. This should be carried out in the autumn, because it is then that the long shoots of roses such as the Hybrid Perpetuals – the family with which pegging down is likely to be most necessary – will have reached their maximum length. About 6in (15cm) of the tips should be removed as they will be soft and unlikely to ripen, and then the rest eased gently over and down towards the ground. One can only judge by feel how far they will go without undue strain, for the last thing that one wants to happen is for them to kink or even snap off. The ends are tied to wooden or metal pegs which are driven into the ground, and these must be long enough for a really firm anchorage. There will, at least until the canes have adapted (or resigned) themselves to their new positions, be quite a strain on them.

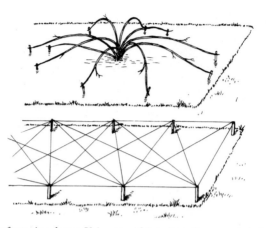

Two kinds of pegging down. Using pegs driven into the ground to tie the tips of the rose canes to (*top*), and the use of a frame formed by wires strung between short wooden stakes.

By careful arrangement of the bowed canes it will be possible to cover a complete bed of Hybrid Perpetuals reasonably evenly, with the canes of the different roses overlapping each other as long as they are not actually rubbing together. No pruning need be done, though awkward side shoots that might otherwise dig into the ground, or with their thorns cause damage to others, should be shortened as necessary and the rest have their tips removed.

An alternative to the use of actual pegs is to drive short stakes into the bed at regular intervals of perhaps 3ft (90cm) and with about 1ft (30cm) of their length above ground level. Galvanised wire (held in place by staples) is then strung from the top of one stake to the next, right round the outside of the bed, and then across it backwards and forwards until all the stakes are joined together in a crisscross pattern. The rose canes can then very easily be tied down to the wire frame you have made, and though setting it up in the first instance involves a certain amount of extra work, you will spend less time in future years than you would if using pegs.

*Dealing with suckers*

Many people find it very difficult to identify suckers. Well, I have some good news for them. It can be much more difficult still with some of the old roses, particularly the species, because the root-stock (assuming one has been used) will be a form of species itself and that standby of sucker identification, seven leaflets to each leaf, cannot apply because your wild rose may well have seven or even more itself. In passing, it should be said that this is not, in any case, ever an infallible guide.

However, it is quite possible that species for gardens will be supplied on their own roots, in which case there can be no suckers of another rose and hence no problem. If he is asked, your supplier will tell you what his practice is before you order, but if you do not find out beforehand it is not difficult to tell after the roses arrive. Canes of a budded rose will be growing from the budding union in the side of the neck of the stock. This is the straight part, about the thickness of a thumb just above the roots themselves, and the point where the top-growth of the rootstock rose has been cut away should be clearly visible immediately above where the new canes have sprouted. Then you must resign yourself to the fact that suckers are going to be at least a possibility. If, however, you are still in doubt and find suckers from roses that have already been planted, gently probe and scrape away at the surrounding earth with a trowel to find out just where they come from. If one is growing from the neck of the stock below the budding union or from the roots themselves, a sucker it will be. Give it a sharp tug and it should come away, together with any dormant buds clustering at its base. This is the only way really to get rid of it, for cutting would simply be the equivalent of pruning and encourage it to try again with renewed vigour. The only real problem may come if a sucker is growing from a spot right under a thick tangle of roots. Finding its source may then be impossible, and all you can do is cut it as far down as you can and hope for the best.

Once you know what a sucker looks like, which is not difficult to learn with a little practice, you will simply be able to pull it away from the roots without doing any underground exploring, but this will only be so if you get on to it straight away, as soon as it shows above the earth. If it is left to develop, it will toughen up and you

167

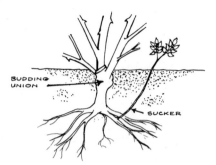

Where a rootstock sucker comes from. If possible, pull it away. Cutting will encourage it to grow more vigorously.

may well have to dig again, not to find it, but so that you can lever it away rather than jerk it free.

As I have referred elsewhere a number of times to roses spreading by suckering, and even said that with hedging roses this can be a good thing, perhaps it would be as well at this point to explain that there are two kinds of sucker. We already know that some rose families, Gallicas and Spinosissimas among them, send out suckers or runners as a natural way of increasing themselves, if they are on their own roots or if they are planted more deeply than usual so that roots can sprout from some of the buried top-growth. This is one kind of sucker, but not the kind you find coming from the rootstock of a budded plant. Here the roots are simply frustrated with having to beaver away in the darkness all the time. They want to show their faces above the earth and produce flowers and leaves, which will be at the expense of the cultivated rose. If they are allowed to get away with it, the much tougher stock, and it is because of its toughness that it has been used in the first place, will gradually take over. Your variety will weaken and fade away.

The type of sucker by which a rose spreads itself usually has fine, hair-like roots attached. If a short portion is chopped off in the autumn and planted elsewhere, you will have a new rose in a few years time. Other than buying them, this is probably the easiest way of increasing your number of roses, though the new ones will be of a variety which you already have. You are, in effect, taking a cutting on which the roots have already begun to grow naturally, so that they will be that much quicker to establish in the

168

ground. Do not forget, however, that the new plant will itself eventually start spreading out once more, sending its own runners far and wide.

### Confining a suckering rose

With the smaller Spinosissimas, one completely foolproof way of doing this is not to plant them in a rose bed at all. I have never seen them grown as tub roses though I can see no reason why they should not be used in this way – bearing in mind the rather limited flowering season – but what I had in mind was a dry-stone wall that has a planting trough built into the top of it. They will not mind the probably rather dry and possibly impoverished soil conditions there, and in time the suckers will find their way through the wall crevices and send out flowering shoots in the most unexpected places. They will look enchanting and can do no harm to anyone.

If, however, you have no such wall and in any case were thinking of using them elsewhere, the best thing is to plant them in a drainpipe. Not the kind of pipe that takes the water down from our roof gutters, but rather a section perhaps 2–3ft (60cm–1m) long and 1ft (30cm) or more in diameter, of the kind of pipe that

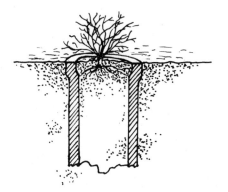

Confining a rose that spreads naturally by suckering in an old drainpipe.

carries sewage away under the streets. A builders' merchant or the yard of a demolition contractor may well have an old, discarded section you can use, though it should not be so damaged as to have holes in its sides. Bury this vertically in the soil with its top rim just showing, plant your rose in this, and defy it to get out. A polythene-lined pit is the only other possibility, but it must have drainage holes punched in the bottom. These holes would really only be effective on very light soil, and there would always be a possibility of the suckers finding them.

## Taking cuttings

As there are many thousands of them I have not raised every single variety of shrub rose from cuttings, so I cannot say that every one can be increased in this way. However, I have been successful with representatives of every group and there is no reason to think that others would present unforeseen difficulties. Some, of course, do get going more quickly than others after they have rooted, most of the species and the ramblers being especially quick off the mark. But with the slower ones this cannot be considered as the quickest way of achieving full-sized bushes. They will take a number of years to build up, but against this they will not have cost you anything, you will have had the excitement of creating something, and you will never have rootstock suckers to plague you.

The method of taking cuttings is exactly the same for all roses. Any time during late summer and the first months of autumn, provided that it is not in the middle of a long dry spell, choose an unoccupied corner of the garden which is open and airy, but is lightly shaded during the hottest part of the day. If you are taking cuttings from a number of different roses, open up as many slits in the earth as may be necessary by pushing a spade down to a depth of just over 6in (15cm) and working it back and forth. If your soil is light and sandy, that is probably all the preparation you will need, but if it is on the heavy side, or even middle of the road, sprinkle some sand along the bottom of the slit to encourage rooting. If the soil is very heavy, perhaps almost the consistency of Plasticine, it will be advisable actually to dig a narrow trench of the same depth as the slit, and with one vertical side. The bottom of the trench should then be covered with about half an inch (15mm) of sand.

Taking cuttings. A cutting ready for planting (*left*), and cuttings inserted in a shallow trench before filling in.

Take the cuttings from substantial shoots of ripened wood of the current season's growth. If the thorns snap off readily it should be about right, and long shoots can be cut into lengths of 9in (23cm) or thereabouts. Make the cuts cleanly just below a leaf axil bud at the bottom, and just above one at the top. Leave the top two or three leaves in place, but remove the rest and also the thorns. Hormone rooting powder may give quicker and surer results, and if you do decide to use it, moisten the bottom of each cutting, dip it into the powder, tap off any excess, and push the cuttings into the prepared slit in the earth about 6in (15cm) apart and so that about two thirds of each is below the surface. If you have dug a trench, place the cuttings upright against the vertical side and, since the trench is 6in (15cm) deep, you will also have two thirds of their length below ground when it is filled in and gently firmed afterwards. With the slit, simply tread along each side so as to push the earth together again. Water well and keep watering for the first few weeks if you have a dry spell. Do not be alarmed when the leaves die off after a time, leaving just small twigs sticking up from the ground. This is a natural process. Refirm the ground with gentle pressure of the foot after frost, which can loosen the earth.

Even if you only want to reproduce one of each rose, it is as well to put in two or three cuttings of it. If one should not take, the chances are that the other two will form roots, but if you only have one to start with you will have lost a year if it dies off. You may end up with more plants than you want, but I have never had difficulty in finding friends who welcome them.

During the first winter after planting a callus will form at the base of each cutting, and in spring this will sprout the first hair-like roots. Above ground there should be signs of life, too, the first few small shoots and leaves. Later, if things are going well, flower buds may form, and while it is tempting to see the magic of these early blooms it is better to pinch the buds out as soon as they are seen. At this stage all growing energy should go into building up the plant itself and not be squandered on decoration. Keep watering if the soil shows signs of drying out.

Late the following autumn the new roses can be moved to their permanent homes, but they must be handled gently as the roots will still be very fragile. Do not forget when lifting them that, because of the length of the cutting, they may branch out fully 6in (15cm) below soil level. Though the plant itself may look tiny, a hand trowel may not be large enough to loosen the soil sufficiently for the rooted end of the cutting to be removed without pulling some of them off. Gentle easing out with a spade is advised, especially on heavy soil.

## Chapter 19

# Seeing, Buying and Further Delving

HAVING spoken a number of times about seeing the larger roses before you buy them, and indeed the smaller ones too, to make sure that they do not turn out bigger than expected, here are a few notes on where you can do it. You can not only see the roses themselves to discover whether or not you like them, but also find out how best they can be used in a multitude of different settings and garden designs. A word of warning, however, before you set out for any of the gardens mentioned.

Not all of them are open to the general public all of the time. With some, access may be restricted to certain days or to specific times every day, or even to members of a society that owns the gardens. Yet others can only be viewed by appointment with the owner, and though I could give some of these details here, they can be changed from time to time and out of date information would be worse than useless. However, in the United Kingdom at least, it is not too difficult to save a wasted journey, for each year publications appear under such titles as *Gardens Open to the Public*, which contain full information about how to get to each garden and at what times it is best to go. If you belong to the National Trust,which has in its care a number of gardens with shrub rose collections, you will already have all the information you need in the publications issued to members. The same applies to members of the Royal National Rose Society and the Royal Horticultural Society and a number of others.

In the British Isles, first and foremost for a visit should come the Rose Society's gardens near St Albans in Hertfordshire. There roses of every imaginable kind and from every period, something like 900 varieties apart from brand new ones in the Trial Grounds, make up one of the most comprehensive collections in the world, well grown, well displayed, and well labelled. Members can get in free, the public on payment at the gate. Or, even closer to the capital, in it in fact, is London's own Queen Mary's Rose Garden in Regent's Park, where there are more modern roses than old, but it is surprising how many shrub roses you can find as you wander round. The same can be said of the Royal Horticultural Society's gardens at Wisley in Surrey. There is a special old garden and shrub rose area and several more borders devoted exclusively to them, but a great many others can be come on unexpectedly in what is not intended to be primarily a rose garden.

In Hampshire Mottisfont Abbey, not far from Winchester, has in a very large walled garden the special National Trust collection of roses predominantly from the Victorian and Edwardian periods, while not far away is Hillier's Nursery and Arboretum, with many unusual species and old garden ones as well. Moving across the country to Kent, a visit to Sissinghurst Castle, another property managed by the National Trust, will enable you to see what is probably the best example of how a profusion of old and modern roses can be used in conjunction with other plants and man-made garden features – walls, arches and so on – to make a harmonious whole.

For those living further north, there is the comparatively new old rose garden at Castle Howard, interesting now, but with a few years yet to go to reach maturity. Across the Pennines and the Irish Sea, in Ulster, is the City of Belfast Rose Trial Gardens, which also has a fairly new but still expanding collection. Long-established and both National Trust, Rowallane and Mount Stewart are over there, too, and well worth a visit.

Others to see are Savill Gardens near Windsor, Clivedon (NT) near Maidenhead for tree-climbing ramblers, Rosemoor Gardens near Torrington in Devon, Kingston Russell House in Dorset, and Montacute House (NT) and Tintinhull (NT), both in Somerset. A little further north in Gloucestershire Hidcote Manor (NT) and Kiftsgate Court are almost next door to each other. More at random, in Lincolnshire there is Gunby Hall (NT), in Northumberland Wallington near Morpeth, in Oxfordshire Buscott Park, especially for Hybrid Musks, Lime Kiln in Suffolk, and Charleston Manor and Nymans (NT) in Sussex. These are only a selection of some of the best from a very much larger total, but at least they are well spread about. Even if only one is in easy reach, visit it, but better still make a pilgrimage to all of them. You will pass others on the way.

For those on holiday abroad, France has two wonderful old rose gardens, one in and one very near Paris, La Roseraie de l'Hay-les-Roses and the Parc de Bagatelle Roseraie. Further south towards the sun La Roseraie d'Orléans has a unique collection of old ramblers in the area where so many of them were first raised. East Germany may not be as accessible to all as it might be, but Sangerhausen Rosarium is there, one of the oldest in the world and one of the most comprehensive. Its 6,500 different varieties and wild roses number among them many which cannot be seen anywhere else. There are, for instance, one hundred and forty different Gallicas.

Much further afield, unless of course you live there, the United States, like Europe, has some interesting old and modern shrub rose collections. The American Rose Centre at Shreveport in Louisiana, headquarters of the American Rose Society, is still being developed and the emphasis is on landscaping different types of site with roses of every kind. Hershey Rose Gardens and Arboretum in Pennsylvania, the Huntington Botanical Gardens, with the largest collection of Tea roses in the United States, the Park of Roses in Columbus, Ohio, Lakeside Rose Garden in Fort Wayne, Indiana (4,000 ramblers), Marquette Park Rose Garden, Chicago, Descano Rose Garden, California, Lake Harriet Park Rose Garden, Minneapolis, Secrest Arboretum in Wooster, Ohio, and DAR Rose Garden, Philadelphia, form what is a very random sample of the total that can be visited. Canada has Butchart Gardens in British Columbia and the Centenial Rose Garden which forms a part of the Royal Botanical Gardens complex at Hamilton, Ontario.

So much for seeing; how about buying? There are many of the bigger general rose nurseries which stock a limited but reasonably representative number of shrub rose varieties. They are useful to start you off, but the time will come when you want to move on to something rather more out of the usual run. Below is a list of some of the specialists, who should, between them, be able to satisfy most needs. If they do not have what you want, keep trying. Someone, somewhere will have it, and tracking down an elusive old rose is like following up the clues in a detective story. Only the frustration of Odysseus trying to get back to Greece after the Trojan War could match that of a rose-grower time after time meeting a dead end, but nothing in gardening can beat the exhilaration when success at last comes.

If you are thinking of buying from an overseas nursery, bear in mind that there are likely to be rules and regulations to be complied with for the importing of any plant. Your local Customs and Excise office should be able to tell you what you must do.

*David Austin Roses* Albrighton, Shropshire, England.
*Peter Beales Roses* Intwood Nurseries, Swardeston, Norwich, England.
*Hillier and Sons* Winchester, Hampshire, England.
*George Longley and Sons* Berengrave Nurseries, Rainham, Kent, England.
*Moon Mountain Nursery* Saskatoon, Saskatchewan, Canada.
*V. Petersen's Planteskole* Plantevej 3, Løve, 4270 Høng, Denmark.
*Roses of Yesterday and Today* 802, Brown's Valley Road, Watsonville, California 95076, USA.
*John Scott* The Royal Nurseries, Merriott, Somerset, England.
*Sunningdale Nurseries* Windlesham, Surrey, England.
*Melvin E. Wyant* Johnny Cake Ridge, Mentor, Ohio 44060, USA.

To find out more and ever more about the roses you grow or want to grow, their fascinating history, the legends they have given rise to, the experiences of others who have grown them from the Greek and Roman periods onwards, what can one do? In one sense America could be said to be better off than almost any country, for there they have Heritage Roses, a society run by old rose enthusiasts and with a nationwide membership. A small magazine, with the same name as the society itself, is circulated four times a year, and conventions and other gatherings of members are organised. It is open to, and welcomes, overseas members, but their participation in the events must of necessity be limited.

Nothing similar exists in the United Kingdom, but membership of the Royal National Rose Society – to which anyone at all who has roses in their garden should belong – will bring with it, in addition to access to the Society's own gardens, the yearly *Rose Annual* in which there are always articles on some aspect of shrub rose growing. Then there are other helpful Society publications such as *Roses – A Selected List of Varieties*, and membership of other national associations such as the American Rose Society or those of France, Germany, Canada and Australia brings similar advantages. The shows, symposia and other events they all organise will put you in touch with people whose interests are yours.

Apart from this there are books to read, and here the field is rich even if you yourself must be rich as well if you want to own a number of them. Otherwise a good horticultural library is the answer, and here once more membership of the Rose Society or of the Royal Horticultural Society will help, for both have fine collections of rose books. But there is really nothing like having them yourself so that you can study them or just browse as and when you feel like it, and there are a good many that you can get quite easily. However, a very large number of the older ones have long been out of print and their value as collectors' items is increasing year by year, so that purchase will mean for the prudent a glance at the balance shown on their cheque stubs before splashing out. Apart from their interest, they will, of course, be an investment; build slowly, one at a time, and savour them at leisure.

In giving a few pointers to some of the best, perhaps I should start with those published since 1900 and then move backwards in time. These will probably be the easiest to find, and though quite a lot of them are now out of print, the prices will – unless they were high to start with – not be quite so steep. In 1978, Heyden of London and Philadelphia issued facsimile editions of a number of the old ones, but, welcome as these may be for research, they are not the same as having the real thing – if you can get it. However, where titles are given in what follows, a note has been added if a facsimile edition is available.

Using the authors' names as our point of reference rather than the titles (sometimes duplicated over the years) and taking them in alphabetical order, E.A. Bunyard's *Old Garden Roses* (Country Life, London, 1936. Facsim. 1978) starts us off. Here is one of the classic books on the old roses and for many years it was considered the standard work. Later research has revealed errors or at least areas of doubt, but this could be said about every rose book ever written. Bunyard was a nurseryman and a scholar, and in most ways cannot be faulted. There are black and white illustrations only, but plenty of them. Millar Gault and Patrick Synge's *Dictionary of Roses in Colour* (Ebury Press and Michael Joseph, London, 1971) on the other hand has colour photographs of very high quality of over 500 roses old and new, or at least new in 1971. Ideal as an aid to identification of unknown varieties, and there are detailed descriptions of the roses by two of Britain's leading authorities.

It is that little bit embarrassing to have two of my own books appear so early in the list, but the alphabet must be, as it has been before, the whipping boy. Modesty should, I suppose, have made me boot them aside, but on the other hand I would not have written them if I did not think I had something of value to say. Anyway, there has already been mention enough of *Shrub Roses for Every Garden* (Collins, London, 1973), but *The Book of the Rose* (Macdonald Futura, London, 1980) I have so far managed to keep from mentioning. An extensive coverage of history, over 1,000 variety descriptions, a tour of rose gardens of the world, cultivation, hybridising – every aspect of roses and rose growing, in fact – and with colour paintings of over one hundred carefully selected roses from the earliest times to the present day by Donald Myall, a number of which have rarely, if ever, been painted before. A little earlier, in 1978, came Jack Harkness's *Roses* (Dent, London), the author a nurseryman (retired), a leading hybridist and a most entertaining writer whose knowledge of roses old and new must be unrivalled in the world today. Original thinking, a real love for and an encyclopedic knowledge of the rose comes over on every page.

*Hillier's Manual of Trees and Shrubs* (paperback, Hillier, Winchester, 1970, and hardback, David and Charles, Newton Abbot, 1972) is basically a vast nursery catalogue, but it is a great deal more than that, being a treasurehouse of information about the thousands of shrubs it covers. Roses old and new are part of it, with a particularly good coverage of wild roses. E.E. Keays is the American author of *Old Roses* (Macmillan, New York, 1935. Facsim. 1978), the strength of this book being its account of roses of the nineteenth century.

The next book, or rather the latest version of it, puts me in a quandary. The late J.H. McFarland was responsible for the series of books *Modern Roses 1–7*, which appeared at intervals between 1930 and 1969 and formed an international checklist giving the raiser, parentage, date of introduction and a brief description of all roses in cultivation throughout the major countries of the world. It is and was a standard work of reference and, considering the difficulties of compilation, on the whole very accurate. In 1980 *Modern Roses 8* appeared, and it is sad to have to say that there are far too many errors in the new material. Best in view of this to find a second-hand copy of no. 7 or even one of the earlier ones, though they will only take you up to 1969 – not too much of a drawback if it is the old roses you wish to check on.

The Rev. Joseph Pemberton's *Roses: Their History, Development and Cultivation* (Longman Green, London) first appeared in 1908 and so just comes into our first batch of books. Pemberton was both a clergyman and a nurseryman, and has much of interest to say based on practical observation of an enormous number of roses. A charming frontispiece in colour of the Dog Rose, and other illustrations in black and white. Roy E. Shepherd's *History of the Rose* (Macmillan, New York, 1954. Facsim. 1978) in many cases gives a stimulating new slant to established thinking, a small instance of which is his theory that R. *tomentosa* may have been the Red Rose of Lancaster rather than R. *gallica officinalis* which usually (and I think more plausibly) lays claim to that distinction. Shepherd is particularly comprehensive on the wild roses. Nancy Steen's *The Charm of Old Roses* (Herbert Jenkins, London, 1966) combines much history and rose lore with shrub rose growing in New Zealand, based on her collection built up from roses brought from Europe by early settlers. Beautiful colour photographs of many of them.

And so we come, as any such survey must, to Graham Thomas's three books, *The Old Shrub Roses* (1955), *Shrub Roses of Today* (1963), and *Climbing Roses Old and New* (1965). Originally appearing under the imprint of Phoenix House, London, later editions bear that of Dent, London, and all old rose lovers owe an incalculable debt to the scholarship and years of painstaking research that have gone into this trio. I cut my old rose teeth on them as thousands of other people must have done, admiring as they read the beautiful watercolours by the author which are used as illustrations. The paintings by Alfred Parsons illustrating Ellen Willmott's *The Genus Rosa* (John Murray, London, 1914) are also timeless, though the text of her treatise on the wild roses of the world, still with its own fascination, is in many ways outdated. And finally, before we move back to the books of the 1900s, mention must be made of *The Complete Rosarian* (Hodder and Stoughton, London, 1971). The author, Norman Young, was nothing if not an original thinker, though one may not always share his views on certain aspects of rose history and other matters. Nevertheless one must respect them as they are not always easy to disprove with absolute conviction, and they do make one think, which is a considerable achievement for any author. Always entertaining and obviously the result of much patient research, the only thing one could really quarrel with, if on the lookout for cultural information, is the use of the word 'complete' in the title. For there is none.

The period which roughly coincided with Queen Victoria's reign produced many worthwhile books which have an historical significance to us now that they did not, of course, have when they were written. In describing the roses that they knew and grew, the authors were giving what at the time was the very latest information. This, in addition to its usefulness in increasing our store of knowledge of the past, now has an old-world charm.

Once again taking them in alphabetical order by author's name, first comes Robert Buist's *The Rose Manual* (Lippincott, Grambo, Philadelphia, 1844. Facsim. 1978). Written by a Scottish nurseryman who emigrated to the United States and aimed at his own customers, it has particular reference to roses suitable for the eastern part of the USA. Coming from this side of the Atlantic, the Rev. H.H. D'Ombrain's *Roses for Amateurs* (The Bazaar, 1887) was written by one of a group of clergymen who seemed to dominate (benevolently, of course) the rose scene in the nineteenth century, while we return over the sea for H.B. Ellwanger's *The Rose* (Dodd-Mead, New York, 1882) with nearly 1,000 roses described. The Rev. A. Foster-Melliar is the second of our rose-writing clerics, and his book *The Book of the Rose* (Macmillan, London, 1894) is rather more heavy going than most of the others and almost obsessively concerned with growing roses for exhibition (Hybrid Perpetuals at that period), so one does at least learn a good deal about them. Mrs C.F. Gore in her *The Book of Roses, or The Rose Fancier's Manual* (Colborn, London, 1838. Facsim. 1978) deals with the vast numbers of roses popular in France early in the century and she drew extensively on French sources for her writing. Shirley Hibberd covers a later period from the 1860s onwards with the various reprints of *The Rose Book* (Groombridge, London, 1864), the title being changed after a while to *The Amateur's Rose Book*. He was a snob. Small gardens were almost beneath his notice, and his attitude to them makes amusing reading now.

Samuel Reynolds Hole, Canon of Rochester, was as we know one of the prime movers in popularising the use of the rose in every garden, large or small. We can see grateful greenfly holding memorial services to him each year on our bushes, and his *A Book About Roses* (Blackwood, Edinburgh, 1874) reprinted so many times and so quickly that it went through the bookshops without touching the shelves. Amusing and very definite in its views, it is not, except incidentally, a book of instruction, but it is a highly entertaining period piece.

Gertrude Jekyll and Edward Mawley's *Roses for English Gardens* (Country Life, London) was actually published in 1902, so it is a bridge between our first two eras. Its main aim is to show how roses should be used to form part of an overall gardening scheme – Miss Jekyll was a pioneer of the idea – rather than being planted entirely on their own, and there are an incredible number of black and white photographs to illustrate her points. An interesting social sidelight on the period at which she was writing is a section of the book on English gardens on the Riviera.

Samuel Parsons' *Parsons on the Rose* (Orange-Judd, New York), W. Prince's *Manual of Roses* (Clark, New York) and Thomas Rivers' *The Rose Amateur's Guide* (Longman Green, London) came out in 1869, 1846 and 1837 respectively, the second two written by nurserymen, one American and one English. Rivers' book is really a supplement to his catalogue, but none the worse for that.

I have after all deviated marginally from the alphabet in putting William Paul's *The Rose Garden* (Kent, London, 1848. Facsim. 1978) last in the Victorian group, as it is fitting to reach a climax with the one that is probably the best of all. Yet another nurseryman author, almost unbelievably Paul wrote his book when he was only twenty-five. Going back to the classical sources, he produced a comprehensive and learned history and a very practical book as well. The early editions had colour plates, later dropped for economic reasons, which perhaps gives me a fellow feeling for him. All editions have charming black and white engravings, both instructional and decorative.

And so we come to the last two books in this necessarily brief roundup. Both are very rare collectors' items which are unlikely to be found, let alone seen, by most of us outside a library. The first is Mary Lawrance's *A Collection of Roses From Nature* of 1799, which contains ninety of her etchings, hand-coloured in the book, and forming a wonderful record of the roses she knew. Secondly there is P. J. Redouté's *Les Roses*, of which I have already sketched in the background and given some details in an earlier chapter. Selections of the plates have been well reproduced from time to time in volume form, notably by Ariel Press in 1954 and 1956, and more recently by Schutter of Belgium. However, the price of the latter, which is a complete facsimile edition, still runs well into four figures. No one has a spare copy, I suppose?

This final chapter really followed the trail that I followed myself. I am certainly not at the end of it yet, and such is its fascination I hope that I never will be. There is always something new to discover. I hope that others will enjoy following it as much as I have. *Bon voyage*.

# Short List

OBVIOUSLY all the roses described in this book can be considered my personal choice or they would not be included, but for a beginner with shrub roses there may well be too many, making the choice of a few to start with difficult. This list of what I consider to be the finest of all reduces the total and so may help, which is not to say that the other roses are not to be recommended as no two enthusiasts will ever agree as to the best. In trying to make it a highly selective choice one's mind moves like a metronome, backwards and forwards, weighing the merits of one rose against another, and once again personal preferences inevitably play a part. About one third of the roses in the book are in this list. No one should, I think, be disappointed in any of them.

**Species and near relatives**

Canary Bird
Complicata
R. × *dupontii*
R. *ecae*
R. *fedtschenkoana*
Frühlingsgold
Frühlingsmorgen
R. × *harisonii* ('Harison's Yellow')
Marguerite Hilling
R. *moyesii* 'Geranium'
Nevada
R. × *paulii rosea*
R. *rubrifolia*
R. *spinosissima altaica*
Stanwell Perpetual

**Gallicas**

Belle de Crécy
Cardinal de Richelieu
Charles de Mills
Du Mâitre d'Ecole
Empress Josephine
Gloire de France
Officinalis
President de Sèze
Rosa Mundi
Tuscany Superb

**Damasks**

Celsiana
Ispahan
La Ville de Bruxelles
Madame Hardy
St Nicholas

## Albas

R. ×*alba maxima*
Celestial ('Céleste')
Félicité Parmentier
Königin von Danemarck

## Centifolias

Centifolia
Chapeau de Napoléon
De Meaux
Fantin-Latour
Petite de Hollande
Tour de Malakoff

## Moss roses

Common Moss
Henri Martin
James Mitchell
Nuits de Young
William Lobb

## China roses

Comtesse du Cayla
Hermosa
Mutabilis
Old Blush

## Bourbons and Portlands

Blairii No. 2 (B)
Commandant Beaurepaire (B)
Ferdinand Pichard (B)
La Reine Victoria (B)
Madame Ernst Calvat (B)
Madame Isaac Pereire (B)
Madame Pierre Oger (B)
Comte de Chambord (P)
Jacques Cartier (P)

## Hybrid Perpetuals

Baronne Prévost
Georg Arends
Mrs John Laing
Paul Neyron
Reine des Violettes
Roger Lambelin•

## Rugosas

Blanc Double de Coubert
Fru Dagmar Hastrup
Max Graf
Roseraie de l'Hay
Sarah Van Fleet
Scabrosa

## Hybrid Musks

Ballerina
Buff Beauty
Moonlight
Penelope
Pink Prosperity
Vanity

## Polyantha types

Bloomfield Abundance
Cécile Brunner
The Fairy
Little White Pet
Nathalie Nypels
Yesterday

## Modern shrub roses

Aloha
Chinatown
Clair Matin
Constance Spry
Erfurt
Fred Loads

Fritz Nobis
Golden Wings
Iceberg
Kathleen Ferrier
Lavender Lassie
Sally Holmes
Scarlet Fire

**Ramblers**

Albéric Barbier
Bobbie James
Félicité et Perpétue
Francis E. Lester

François Juranville
R. *longicuspis*
Rambling Rector
Ramona

**Climbers**

Altissimo
R. *banksiae lutea*
Cécile Brunner, Cl.
Gloire de Dijon
Madame Grégoire Staechelin
Madame Alfred Carrière
New Dawn

# General Index

186

# GENERAL INDEX

# Index of Roses

References to principal entries are in **bold** type and those to colour plates are in *italic*.

# INDEX OF ROSES

Marguerite Hilling  33
Marie Pavié  106
Marjorie Fair  118
Max Graf  91, 94, 146
Meg  135
Meg Merrilees  36
Mermaid  15, 136, 101, 143, *Pl.14*
Moonlight  98, 101, 143, *Pl.14*
Moss, Damask  64
Mousseline  68
Mozart  99
Mrs John Laing  14, 84, 87
Mrs Herbert Stevens, Climbing  137, *Pl.16*
Mutabilis  72, *Pl.8*

Nathalie Nypels  107
Nevada  25, 32, 33, 141, *Pl.2*
New Dawn  137
Nova Zembla  91, 94
Nuits de Young  20, 68
Nur Mahal  102
Nymphenburg  118

Officinalis  41, 46, 82, 179, *Pl.1*
Old Blush  70, 73, *Pl.1*
Old Pink Moss  66
Ormiston Roy  39

Parsons' Pink China  70, 73
Paul Crampel  104, 107
Paul Neyron  87, *Pl.10*
Paul's Himalayan Musk Rambler  127
Paul's Lemon Pillar  137, *Pl.16*
Pax  98, 102
Peace  108, 118
Péllison  68
Penelope  98, 99, 102, 143, *Pl.14*
Perle des Panachées  20, 42, 47, *Pl.4*
Perle d'Or  70, 108
Persian Yellow  23, 30, 31
Petite de Hollande  60, 62
Phoebe's Frilled Pink  93
Pink Grootendorst  95, *Pl.13*
Pink Perpétue  145
Pink Prosperity  102, 143
Pompon de Paris  73
Portland Rose, the  82, *Pl.8*
Poulsen's Park Rose  119
President de Sèze  47
Prince Camille de Rohan  20, 88
Prince Charles  80
Prosperity  102, 143

Quatre Saisons  49, 52, 64, 70, 75, 179
Quatre Saisons Blanc Mousseux  49, 64
Queen Elizabeth  119, 141
Queen of Denmark  57

Radway Sunrise  120
Rambling Rector  127, 141, *Pl.15*

Ramona  127
Raubritter  32, 120
Rayon d'Or  30
Red Cherokee  127
Red Rose of Lancaster  18, 46
Reine des Violettes  15, 20, 85, 88, *Pl.10*
Reveil Dijonnais  16
Robert le Diable  20, 62
Roger Lambelin  85, 88, *Pl.10*
Rosa × *alba incarnata*  56
    × *alba maxima*  25, 26, 55, 141, 149
    × *alba semi-plena*  15, 55, *Pl.5*
    *arvensis*  122
    *banksiae lutea*  131
    *banksiae lutescens*  131
    *brunonii* 'La Mortola'  124
    *californica*  27
    *californica plena*  27
    *canina*  21
    × *cantabrigiensis*  27
    × *centifolia cristata*  61
    × *centifolia muscosa*  66
    *chinensis* 'Major'  71, *Pl.8*
    *chinensis semperflorens*  74
    *chinensis viridiflora*  26
    *corymbifera*  25, 54
    × *damascena* 'Trigintipetala'  52, *Pl.5*
    × *damascena versicolor*  49, 53
    × *dupontii*  15, 28
    *ecae*  28
    *eglanteria*  35
    *farreri*  29
    *farreri persetosa*  29
    *fedtschenkoana*  22, 29
    *filipes* 'Kiftsgate'  125
    *foetida*  29, 30
    *foetida bicolor*  23, 29, 30
    *foetida persiana*  23, 30, 31, *Pl.1*
    *foliolosa*  17
    × *francofurtana*  46
    *forrestiana*  31
    *gallica*  26
    *gallica officinalis*  41, 46, 82, 179, *Pl.1*
    *gallica versicolor*  26, 47
    × *harisonii*  31
    *hugonis*  27, 28
    *hugonis* 'Headleyensis'  31
    *humilis*  39
    *longicuspis*  126
    *luciae*  122
    *lucida*  39
    × *macrantha* hort.  28, 32
    × *macrantha* 'Lady Curzon'  32
    *monstrosa*  74
    *moyesii*  22, 32, 142
    *moyesii* 'Eos'  33
    *moyesii* 'Geranium'  33, *Pl.2*
    *moyesii* 'Highdownensis'  33, *Pl.2*
    *moyesii* 'Marguerite Hilling'  33
    *moyesii* 'Nevada'  33, *Pl.2*